Keelia !

Make the impossible possible !
Thanks for supporting #EDD.
Be the light
♡

Rachel

Cover photo by Sunshine Velasco
Author photo page 3 by Fifi Fresh
Author biography photo page 137 by Sunshine Velasco
Cover Design and Page Layout by Cheyenne Varner
Edited by AnJu Hyppolite of The Write Gift

All recipes contained in this book were created by Rachel
Bolden-Kramer or adapted from others where noted, except for
Cauliflower Ceviche by Marlene Sanchez, Oakland Scavenger
Salad by Anita de Asis, Struggle Potatoes by Lateefah Simon, and
Heirloom Grits aka Blue Cornmeal by Mari Posa.

My Food Stamps Cookbook
EBT-Priced Radical Nutrition
Copyright © 2017 by Rachel Bolden-Kramer

Printed in the United States of America

First Printing, 2017

ISBN-13: 978-1981983711
ISBN-10: 1981983716
BISAC: Cooking / General

Published by Hip Dhamma, Inc
535 Appian Way Ste 21431
El Sobrante, CA 94820

www.myfoodstampscookbook.com

10 9 8 7 6 5 4 3 2 1

Dedication

My whole life for Issa

Contents

Chapter One

Intro to Food Stamps Cookbook

So here's the deal: You don't need to be a welfare recipient to be on a tight budget. Ever since I graduated from college in 2006, I've been on a super-tight budget, sometimes getting food stamps, sometimes crying about not getting them. And I went to a freaking Ivy League school. The problem is that there is rampant poverty in the United States and having a degree doesn't make you immune to it, especially if you're the first in your family to get a degree. I have countless friends working on doctorates and advanced degrees who are broke as shit. The reality is that a ton of people in the US are trying to figure out how to afford food and live their lives. The number of people getting food stamps was about 45 million in 2016 (SNAPtohealth.org 2016).[1]

Food Stamps, aka Supplemental Nutrition Assistance Program (SNAP), aka Electronic Benefits Transfer (EBT), is a revolutionary program. It is an anti-poverty social welfare program that I love because it means that even if you are broke, in transition, sick, etc., you can still have access to food. When people aren't worried about where their next meal is coming from, the possibility for productivity increases. I have always advocated for my friends and family to apply for benefits when they find themselves in between jobs. Unlike Women, Infants, and Children (WIC), food stamps are not vouchers for specific foods. Food stores that take EBT include retail, wholesale, grocery coops, farmers markets, drugstores, and convenience stores. The prevalence of food stamps compatible marketplaces makes EBT a valuable currency and daily resource for many people.

The reason I took on the project of radicalizing food stamps with the style of diet outlined in this book is because I became aware of a probable, almost certain outcome: Studies show that the longer a person receives food stamps, the greater the risk for poor health.

I fought to change this in my own life by deconstructing the stigma about food stamps and the scarcity thinking that falling within low-income standards meant that I had to consume sub-par, unhealthy foods. As a college student, yoga teacher trainee, nutrition student, and entrepreneur, I harnessed the buying power of my food stamps or my small income, at times, to access superfoods that would give me the power necessary to hustle and stay on the grind. These foods have the added benefits of healing and preventing disease. If we have less disease and discomfort to address, we can spend more time doing what we love.

Food stores that take EBT include retail, wholesale, grocery coops, farmers markets, drugstores, and convenience stores.

[1] www.snaptohealth.org/snap/snap-frequently-asked-questions/#howmany

Luckily, I happened to have developed my approach to nutrition while receiving $200 a month in food stamps.

Fast-forward past surviving the state of the US economy immediately after I attained my fancy bachelor's degree. My struggle with food and budgeting became so much more real when I got pregnant. I was twenty-nine when I found out I would soon become a mom, and I was deep in the hustle as a small business owner of a community yoga studio in BedStuy, Brooklyn. Suddenly, I needed what felt like ten times as much food, as my capacity to work had drastically diminished.

Luckily, I happened to have developed my approach to nutrition while receiving $200 a month in food stamps, so this book reflects that marginal budget. When I became a baby mama (a longer story about letdowns and reclaiming power), my stamps jumped to a whopping $357 plus WIC bennies here and there. During this time I was not turning a profit from my business,

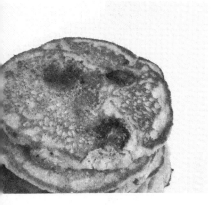

nor was I being supported by the source of my child's paternal DNA. I was suddenly navigating homelessness, financial disaster, and a freaking ruthless custody battle. It's a miracle I even survived to write this book!

The miracle is possible because of the transformation I achieved before all this shit had hit the fan. When I became pregnant, I had been living in the aftermath of disability and had already learned that my food practice was what healed and sustained me. How? Well, that's the basis of radical nutrition. Here is the bottom line: Digestion is the metabolic process that consumes the majority of your energy. When you're struggling and hustling, your energy is what is absolutely necessary to help you push through circumstances. In order to succeed and accelerate your progress, you must minimize energy drain. Please tell me if you have ever successfully accomplished something with the itis! No, you haven't. You tried to fix it with frappuccinos, Red Bull, or some other stimulant, and that just made it worse.

Furthermore, when you have food coma, or you're hangry because what you ate did not sustain you, you're more prone to experience depression and anxiety. I had been diagnosed with clinical anxiety/depression because I survived some real-life fucked up shit and became one of the many humans on this earth with a condition called Post Traumatic Stress Disorder. I never took a single pharmaceutical treatment. I did, however, use a myriad of approaches (e.g. food, herbs, trauma therapies, and traditional healing) to address my symptoms. It is possible to use the tools of radical nutrition to even if you do take medications or must take them. With this approach, your body actually becomes better at everything it does, therefore you may be able to use less of what you are taking medicinally to achieve the benefits you seek.

My Food Stamps Cookbook is a guidebook to eat for the hustle, and I have a few real tips about hustling, too. Plus, I have the realest empowerment philosophy you will ever find because I actually lived my life in the trenches, achieved a freaking bachelor's from Harvard, then went back into the trenches as a trauma survivor. I healed and then got slapped with baby mama drama.

The most powerful truth I learned is that transformation happens at every stage. Every moment of the struggle is a moment for deeper awakening. The most powerful awakening I have had has been supported by the most basic practice for sustaining my human life: **EATING**! You do it all day long, so what better time to give to yourself to **HEAL**?

> EATING! You do it all day long, so what better time to give to yourself to HEAL!

True confession: When I was faced with fighting for the custody of my newborn, I mostly survived on donuts... **ALL. DAY. EVERY. DAMN. DAY**. I lost my pregnancy weight and then gained some back. I was not feeling powerful at all. Yet, today, I am back on the wagon, eating to heal, happily enjoying primary custody of my little girl, and living in a mansion. Yes, a **MANSION**. From homelessness, kidnapping charges, and the donut diet, I transformed it all. I bought a Prius and a castle, and I am living the life of my dreams.

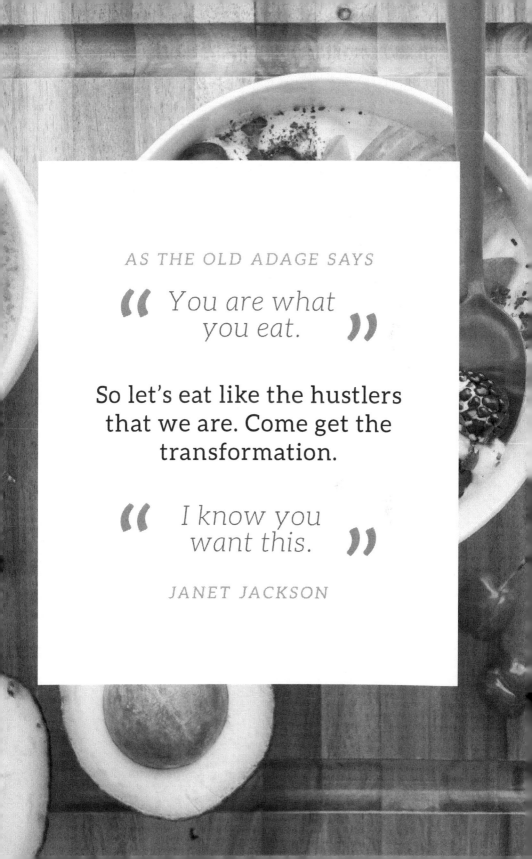

AS THE OLD ADAGE SAYS

" You are what you eat. "

So let's eat like the hustlers that we are. Come get the transformation.

" I know you want this. "

JANET JACKSON

Chapter Two

Radical Nutrition: Revolutionize Your Body

So how do we create revolution on our plates so that we have more energy, less disease, and the power to achieve our dreams? It starts with rethinking the misinformation we have swallowed about the foods we consume and how we eat. For the most part, our bodies are composed of what we were born with and what we have added as we navigate our hectic lives. Some of what we are composed of is toxic chemicals, heavy metals, and the remnants of foods we are addicted to. Revolution means learning how our nature and constructed ways of being influence that next bite we want to take. Damn, this could be a metaphor for life itself!

Radical nutrition is capitalizing on what our bodies do best and our resiliency. Here's something else about radical nutrition: It heals. Because we learn to minimize energy drain and have more power, we get access to our body's own natural life force. This can allow opportunities to address historical diseases that may have gone dormant yet have been consuming our hustle power by creating other sub symptoms like fatigue, pain, or chronic depression, and even doubt. Plus, a whole bunch of melanated and otherwise marginalized peoples have intergenerational trauma lineages in our DNA that can be deployed at any moment to stand in the way of our optimal use of energy. If our food supports us optimally, we can bring awareness to emotional and physical suffering, and not let it take us down! We can actually transform it.

Radical nutrition is capitalizing on what our bodies do best and our resiliency.

Now this is **RADICAL** nutrition. It's not a fad diet or expensive supplement. It is a budget-friendly tactic for creating a new experience in your body. Check out this breakdown:

RADICAL NUTRITION IS	RADICAL NUTRITION IS NOT
Simple	Wasteful
Detoxifying	Weight-loss fad
Environmentally Friendly	Expensive
Healing	Hard to achieve
Inflammation reducing	Dangerous
Safe	
Gentle	
Affordable	

In essence, we will go back to the basics. We will unlearn the profit-driven tactics that have made you addicted to things that aren't even food. We will re-learn the wonders of how our ancestors ate and make them relevant for our times.

Let's review why this is so powerful for raising your energy to hustle and your vibration overall. We increase our vibration by bringing the body into a state of alkalinity or reducing acidity, the cause of inflammation. What are some conditions that are caused by inflammation? Just about any sickness you have or will ever encounter: acne, premenstrual syndrome (PMS), asthma, eczema, Type 2 Diabetes, congestion, indigestion, infertility, tooth decay, and acid reflux (to name a few). These illnesses are all due to acidosis, the over-acidity of the body.

Research now shows that inflammation is the precursor to cancer. Precancerous cells are found waiting to strike around inflammatory tissue in the body. Don't believe me? Ask Dr. Google or an expert at The Center for Mind Body Medicine, where I completed the Food as Medicine Certification Program to become a life coach in radical nutrition for individuals and organizations.

Where else does this information on radical nutrition come from? I learned an incredible amount of wisdom from my sister, Julie R. Brown, whom I met at a meditation retreat in Massachusetts and then studied under in New York. I continued my education with her master teacher, Gil Jacobs, a renegade radical nutrition practitioner also in NYC. It was while working with Gil that I became pregnant, after healing years of debilitating PMS and ovarian cysts. Because of this healing work, I had a miraculously healthy pregnancy, quick birth, and happy baby who loves the food that keeps her healthy.

It was while working with Gil that I became pregnant, after healing years of debilitating PMS and ovarian cysts.

After becoming a mom, I realized I wanted to serve my fellow birthing humans as a full-spectrum doula and birth worker. Watching client after client move from conception through pregnancy, to birth, breastfeeding or not, and parenting, I got to see how the conditions of our lives influence our ability to thrive and birth people who thrive. This urgency showed me just how important it is to have transformative health via food. Furthermore, because maternal and infant mortality rates for marginalized people in the US are deplorable, we need tools that are accessible for reversing these tragedies. Poor US mothers and babies, and all women and babies of African descent, regardless of income and education, are more likely to die or suffer unnecessarily in the US than in 44 other countries in the world. *My Food Stamps Cookbook* can save lives. We can absolutely change the story of suffering by reducing inflammation in our diets and mentalities.

Our food and food system are the places where the most profound transformation can occur. Even people living with the most limited resources can harness the power of food in their lives and invent a completely new possibility for health and the energy to realize their dreams. In doing so, I believe we will create the possibility for a whole, sustainable planet.

Chapter Three

No Cheeto (Not Even in Moderation)!

First, it's time to get rid of everything you should not eat. If you hire me as your radical nutritionist, I'll come to your house and throw away your hot Cheetos. Damn, I used to love those things. But I am cut-throat in the pantry and with good reason. Cheetos are deceptively delicious. I remember when I started to detox from them. I remember the indulgent relapses. Each time I survived the Cheetos relapse, I realized just how powerful the chemicals in food are. Snack foods like Cheetos, Doritos, Ruffles' Sour Cream and Onion (all my early childhood favorites) domesticate our taste buds. Nothing we taste afterward is ever as good.

When you start getting rid of these foods, you aren't really going to love the real food alternatives immediately. You will need some time away from the flavor enhancers that have manipulated your preferences. Trust me, hundreds of people have told me that they just don't like vegetables. You know what I tell them? You are a fucking slave to Frito-Lay. Take your power back! You gotta go Nat Turner on the processed food. It's a literal uprising against your complacent tongue.

Here's the breakdown of how to do it.

1 **Read the whole damn label.** It's on the back. Ignore the calories part. Look at what the eff the top three ingredients are. Then, look at all the other crap you can't even pronounce. What is that shit anyway?

2 **Ignore the words "natural" and "healthy"**, or just assume they are meant to trick you.

3 **Sugar is sugar is sugar.** If it's sweet, it's sugar; and it's acidic, which is inflammatory. I'm not talking about actual real fruits. No drink that is sweet that you can get in the shiny, pretty bottle is in any way good for you or lower in sugar or blah blah blah.

4 **Stop reading crappy articles on the internet** that may have been planted by Monsanto, the company that owns seeds, contaminates our food and water with deadly chemicals, and promotes the big brands we are addicted to stuffing in our pantries and mouths. Anyone can write a stupid article stating that kale is dangerous or skipping breakfast is bad. That doesn't make it true. Skip breakfast, please, and replace it with kale.

5 **Nothing that sits on a shelf for weeks, months, or years, without decaying, is actual food.** Those pretty little honey buns are truly industrial cement. Seriously. Where the eff does industrial cement go after you swallow it? Ask your ancestors on the other side

who died of heart disease. Sorry, not sorry!

6 **There is no such thing as low fat.** Fat is freaking good for you. The low-fat crap is just made out of artificial fat, AKA industrial cement (see above).

7 **Stop acting like meat is an essential part of your diet.** True, it once was great for humans, maybe somewhat. But if you are on the planet now, the meat you are eating is probably factory farmed, eating corn products or its own deceased relatives, living in its own feces, and dead before it gets to the slaughter house. Plus, it's angry that it is living that way and the anger lives in its cells. So yum, you get meat that doesn't contain the essential ingredients that made it nutritional to begin with, because it's been raised so poorly, and it's mad at you for supporting its suffering. Swallow that. Now, there are some good meats. They are either expensive or you are raising them in your backyard. I give you the green light to consume such meats.

8 **Remember that nothing is a genetic disease.** Diabetes does not run in your family. Cancer does not run in your family. You know what runs in your family? People eating garbage and being self-righteous about it at that. Diabetes comes from systemic inflammation. Cancer is the body's response to the morbid accumulation of toxins in your organs. Your food activated the genes for these conditions by creating a shitty environment inside you.

9 **It's never too late to change, BUT the sooner you do, the better.** Look, I grew up on Popeyes and McDonald's, then SlimFast and Snackwell's. It took years off my life. I suffered tremendously from chronic illness, pain, depression, etc. As soon as I brought my awareness to changing my conditions, I had dramatic positive results.

10 DRINK WATER. But not that water. You
gotta hydrate more to make radical change.
But faucet water is mostly contaminated. Flint, anyone?
Think that shit ain't running out your tap? Think again.
One of the most powerful things you can do is change
your drinking water source. Even if it's just a moderate
improvement over what is on tap. By the way, fluoride
actually fucks up momma's placenta. Real talk.

The cheapest approach to detoxifying municipal water
on a simple level (does not remove fluoride) is charcoal
sticks. It's the green way to filter tap water. I ordered it
online at: *https://kishucharcoal.com*

Stop Feeding This to Your Babies (and Yourself) Right Now!

There's no such thing as moderation in this discussion. Sorry. I'm
not gonna let you slowly kill yourself and your babies. Now is the
time to read the labels for real. I can't tell you how many times I
put back the WIC-approved peanut butter brand because it was
hydrogenated, aka trans fats, aka **MURDER**. There is a popular
approach to diet and lifestyle that states that some harmful
things need not be eliminated from the diet, but rather enjoyed in
moderation. Nope, no way. Never. **WHY**? Because cancer.

This is a list of food products that **CANNOT** be consumed, even
in moderation, because of their immediate and cumulative
detrimental effects. If you look closely at the food that is
marketed as "cheap" and affordable for people and families
on a tight budget, this crap is usually in it. And it is delicious
and addictive. In the following discussion, I offer strategies
for how to deal with missing these popular foods as you begin
eliminating them.

Hydrogenated anything

Any oil that is preceded by hydrogenated or partially hydrogenated is to be regarded as the enemy. This is the worst chemically modified oil out there. Historically used in the fat-free craze of the 90s, it has been found to be the cause of pandemic heart disease. What's truly f-ed up about this is it's in almost everything that comes in a neat little package at the bodega or corner store. And it's in popular brands of peanut butter, bread, and cookies, crackers, and most stuff that folks might give their kids for lunch. Yikes! It can also be found in non-dairy creamers, granola bars, and foods that are masquerading as healthy alternatives. It may also appear in candy. Hydrogenated oil is made so that it does not decompose and allows a food product to have longer shelf life, which means more profits for food companies. But if it doesn't decompose on the shelf, it's not breaking down in your body either.

Monosodium glutamate (MSG)

Say goodbye to all Top Ramen and Cup Noodle products. Now. Do it. Trust me. Also disguised as disodium inosinate and disodium guanylate, scientists claim that there are no adverse side effects from consuming glutamate. There are, however, "anecdotal" accounts of adverse reactions to MSG including headaches and allergy-like symptoms or "MSG Symptom Syndrome" which is said to include headache, flushing, sweating, facial pressure or tightness, numbness, heart palpitations, chest pain, nausea, and weakness (Mayo Clinic 2017)[2]. My advice is to consider that these side effects may be occurring. Sometimes we may not be aware of them, but if eliminated and reintroduced after a significant absence, greater awareness may be possible. Outside of broadening your awareness to food reactions, simply consider what foods are most likely to contain MSG. These are usually modified starch

[2] www.mayoclinic.org/healthy-lifestyle/nutrition-and-healthy-eating/expert-answers/monosodium-glutamate/faq-20058196

products with little nutritional benefit. If you make it a practice to cut out MSG, you will eliminate lower quality foods by default, though keep in mind some "natural" food products may also contain MSG derivatives. Stay woke.

Aspartame

This is an artificial sweetener in gum, mints, and diet foods and drinks. It is linked to obesity. Naturally, there will be scientists that say it is completely safe, and that adverse reactions are anecdotal (see above re: MSG). You will have to do your own research to determine where you stand. If you want to save time, just trust me that high-quality, nourishing food sources do not need to have flavor enhancers.

Milk, Flavored Milk Drinks, and Dairy Products

Fuck this shit. Cow milk and cow milk products are for cow babies only! Let's address this y'all. So check out my favorite guide to eating well, *By Any Greens Necessary*, by Tracy Lynn McQuirter. She breaks it down to an audience of Black women who want

to revolutionize their health. Dairy is not the way to go. It does not provide calcium for your bones. It actually contributes to acidity, and then your body responds to neutralize the acidity by leaching minerals from your bones. This is the opposite of what we want. It's in that book. Check it out.

Corn Syrup

This is a very common sweetener that is found prevalently in soda and juices. It is highly addictive to your taste buds.

Most Honey

You gotta do your research here. That honey in the little packets and the cute plastic honey bears may be super denatured honey from China and India. It's poison. There is safe honey – it's local, raw, and available at your local farmer's market, grocery co-op, Trader Joe's (TJs), or from the homegirl down the way with the beekeeping set up. Peep game: When you have high quality honey, you actually get a good, lower glycemic sweetener. I used it frequently in raw recipes, never cooked, to retain the beneficial nutrients.

Olein

This is a super weird Frankenfood dreamed up in an evil laboratory. It arrived on the scene as "olestra" back in the 90s. Even though it was soon found to cause major internal harm to those who consumed it, it is still used in many common snack foods: Pringles.

Artificial Dyes

Not only are they linked to cancer, infertility, and more, why would you want dead food anyway? Remember, the corporate, profit-driven agricultural companies want to hook you on their made-up foods, so they dye them to make them prettier and more eye-catching than something from nature. Some of the dyes to look out for are Red 40, Yellow 5, and Yellow 6.

Moderation Maybe, Still Avoid!

"Natural" juices and smoothies...

like Odwalla, Naked, Bolthouse Farms. Don't buy these because they are pasteurized so there's nothing left of the original nutrients from the fruits and vegetables initially used. It's just not a cost-effective way to use your budget.

Yogurt

Stay away because it is also pasteurized, removing the beneficial probiotics that it is said to contain. Probiotics are actually added after the pasteurization process.

Furthermore, some yogurts contain corn syrup and strange artificial ingredients.

"Whole Grain" breads...

or products that contain artificial ingredients. Just because the label has words that are associated with healthy does not mean that it is actually good for you.

Nuts or seeds that are roasted or cooked in oil

Limit these because the cooked oil is often shady and denatured, or partially hydrogenated, or basically rancid. Gross. Rancid oils are toxic.

Canola Oil

If you want to be a true boss in the radical nutrition world, you will avoid products with this somewhat unnatural oil. There is some debate about how harmful or unharmful it is, which is why I put it here in the medium harm category. Just peep how cheaper food products are loaded with it, and how it costs much less than other cooking oils.

Rancid Oils

For that matter, let's examine those oils sitting on the shelf at your grocery store or in your pantry. Most oil is in a clear bottle. Therefore, it is exposed to light. So it has likely become rancid before you bought it. This goes for vegetable oil (which is actually soybean oil), olive oil, and corn oil. I reference proper oil storage in Appendix B.

Agave

No, it's just as processed as corn syrup. This is total trickery.

So, in summary, you revolutionary health warriors will no longer consume nor feed your children:

Candy

Kit Kat, Milky Way, and Reese's Pieces (My all time faves!) are loaded with hydrogenated oil, corn syrup, dyes, and weird preservatives (reread: industrial cement).

Super flavored chips, Ramen Noodles...

Keep in mind that "ramen" is a type of noodle and can be made healthy. The popular instant, just-add-water ramen noodle brands, unfortunately, have problematic ingredients.

Juice and sodas...

sweetened with artificial sugars.

Chewing gum

with aspartame, sorbitol, and other scary sugars.

Most iced tea products

Arizona and Nestea contain

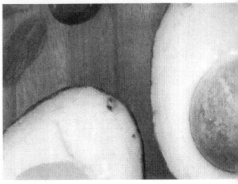

corn syrup or extraordinary levels of sugar.

Convenient baked goods...

at the corner store. Read the labels if you must have them.

Peanut Butter

from Skippy, Jif, or generic store brands because of the bad oil.

The Transitional Foods List

Buy these things instead while you are learning about your new revolutionary approach to eating. It's harm reduction:

Crackers, kettle chips, corn or grain tortilla chips

without lard or hydrogenated oils.

Dark chocolate or candy free of hydrogenated oils and corn syrup.

Breads, tortillas, other baked grains.

Raw, unroasted nuts and seeds. Even roasted or salted nuts are ok, as long as you avoid bad oil.

Fresh fruits and veggies,

organic or not, are still better than Little Debbie.

Natural sodas with cane sugar. Just be aware of how much sugar you consume.

Tea that you can have plain or sweeten yourself

or iced tea drinks without corn syrup and artificial ingredients.

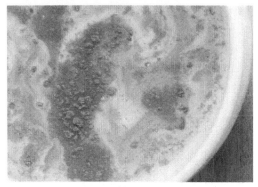

What to Buy

All right, now that I killed your junk food dreams, here's the stuff to replace it with. Generally speaking, you need this:

Good Sugar

Maple syrup, raw honey (non-vegan), coconut sugar, pure raw cane sugar if you have to because of your budget. Awesome sugars like yacon and stevia (leaves, preferably) can get a bit more pricey . You can also use dates and raisins to sweeten teas and smoothies, and to even make desserts.

Good Oil

Olive oil in dark bottles. Coconut oil in glass jars. Soy-free "buttery" spread, which may contain canola, but is less harmful than margarine. Better alternatives are usually coconut butter/oil based and have no canola, dyes, or "natural flavors".

Harm-Reducing Quick Fixes...

Keep a food first aid kit! Cane sugar and/or agave containing granola bars have been life-savers on numerous occasions when I may have whooped my screaming child while she was having a low moment while I too was having a low moment. It's like the Snickers commercial effect where you bite into the candy bar and everything is cheery again. Only this strategy saves you from the ingredients in actual Snickers that I listed in the never ever ever category.

Granola and bars...

made with healthier sugars like maple syrup, honey, coconut sugar, yacon, maybe dat agave, etc.

Yummy crunchy snacks and cereals...

for the babies to crunch on. The best snacks you can find will be free of modified sugars and artificial vitamins (fortified).

Raw food treats...

including nuts, seeds, dried fruit, and of course, fresh fruits and veggies (e.g. carrot sticks, jicama sticks, and cucumber sticks, etc.).

The Dirty Dozen and the Clean Fifteen

You also need a good guide to buying organic vs. conventional produce. There's no sense in wasting your dough at Whole Food (Stamps) on organic avocados when conventional avocados are less expensive and safe to eat. But, you better grab the organic romaine hearts over conventional lettuces at Trader Joe's so you skip the gazillion life-threatening pesticides used to grow leafy greens. Install the Environmental Working Group App or print

Install the Environmental Working Group App or print the "Dirty Dozen, Clean Fifteen" list to find which produce can be safely consumed so you can pay for cheaper conventional watermelon and mangos!

the "Dirty Dozen" and "Clean Fifteen" lists to find which produce can be safely consumed so you can pay for cheaper conventional watermelon and mangos!

Chapter Four

Food (Stamps) As Medicine:
How to Eat for Transformation

This is how to eat for energy and healing. Ok, so you threw out all your crap and replaced it with wholesome goodness! Congrats. But wait, there's more.

You want to hustle harder, right? To get optimal energy toward conquering capitalist heteropatriarchy, you must learn these new food rules. By the way, I am **NOT** a registered dietitian (RD). Though, I have considered becoming one just so I can better subvert the system. The reason I choose not to be indoctrinated into RD education is because it does not give us any revolutionary information. It's fine if you want basic info about protein and carbs and why dairy food is good for you. See the problem? **DAIRY** foods are **TERRIBLE** for you. I'm writing this as I sit in a state-mandated nutrition training session for childcare providers and they are repeating and re-emphasizing serving whole cow's milk to babies as soon as they are twelve months old. **WHAT. THE. FUCK?!?!?!**

Back to radical nutrition. My approach for gaining new energy and ganas in all areas of life asks you to discard most of the garbage you learned about food. For example: overemphasis of protein, breakfast is the most important meal of the day, snack frequently throughout the day, eat rice and beans together, coconut oil is bad for you, eat enriched cereals, fruit is a healthy dessert, rice cereal is good for babies. These are all myths and/ or propaganda created by the big agriculture companies to sell you their surplus and otherwise stuff it into the mouths and communities of low-income people and our children.

Check out the radical approach to eating. Here are the agreements:

Hydration Massive

As soon as you wake, brush your teeth (so you don't swallow all the gunk your body detoxed while you were sleeping), and start drinking water. Warm or room temperature water is the best for encouraging your body to eliminate through the bowels.

You should drink 24-32 ounces of water as soon as you wake up. Start slow and work up to this.

Drink more water throughout the day, but not with food. If you just ate, wait 30 minutes before drinking water, ideally 8-16 ounces at a time. If you just drank some water, wait 30 minutes before you eat food.

PRO TIP

Add a squeeze of lemon juice or a table-spoon of raw apple cider vinegar to the water to blast the toxins out of you. Wink wink. You WILL feel lighter!

23

If you just ate, wait 30 minutes before drinking water, ideally 8-16 ounces at a time. If you just drank some water, wait 30 minutes before you eat food. Prep your vessel to receive the food. From now on, you will not just stuff yourself as soon as you feel hungry. OMG what about when you get that busy momma hangry impulse to scarf all the food scraps your kid left on the table? What if you are faced with a huge spread of free food at a meeting or event? Let's take a moment and talk about how hunger and hangriness feel.

First, recognize that hunger is an emotion, not an indicator of imminent death. Take a moment; feel how hunger presents itself in your body. Do you feel an urgency? A tightening in the stomach? A cloudiness of thoughts and impulses? Just recognize this as the process of hunger communicating in your body. Breathing deeply and hydrating, how soon do these sensations subside? It can be super powerful just to acknowledge that you are feeling hunger.

So before you eat the meal or scraps sitting in front of you, you are going to prep your digestive system with some nice anti-inflammatory dressing: Salad first! You will have salad before eating anything else, except fruit, which I will address next. Salad, or basically any raw leafy greens or water-rich veggies, are the perfect way to revolutionize your digestion. Remember, digestion is the process that consumes the majority of your vital hustle energy. So, we prep the digestive system with an alkaline, water-rich lube to help push everything

PRO TIP

Just like all our other emotions, recognizing and acknowledging them are often all that is required to liberate yourself from them. Try this: "I feel hunger." vs. "I am hungry." Suddenly, hunger has no hold on you and your actions because you are not actually hungry. You are the infinite, life-affirming, master hustler in the game, since birth. You just temporarily feel hungry.

else through rapidly. This will reduce slowdowns and traffic jams.

When food slows and stops, it begins to breakdown and rot where it is stuck. Then it creates gas and inflammation. Now you feel bubble guts, indigestion, and fatigue; and you start making dangerous chemistry experiments in your tummy and intestines. Also, you produce more mucus to help protect you from the inflammation. This is often the precursor of all diseases and discomfort in the body. Our new radical approach to dining works to reduce and prevent illness because it minimizes systemic and chronic inflammation, which is basically the beginning of **ALL** our health problems.

The recipes you'll find in this book's salad and meal prep sections are all geared toward making this transition delicious and easy. If you don't have time to make and eat a salad, you can easily chomp on a romaine heart, red bell pepper, jicama cubes, celery sticks, carrot sticks, or cucumbers. The volume is what matters here. You **MUST** eat a ginormous amount of your water-rich alkaline prep to get optimal results. Think of the size of a salad you would serve at dinner for a family of three. This is the size you want to consume by yourself, especially before a big meal or foods from the more harmful list. And check out the added benefit: With a tummy **FULL** of leaves, you crowd out the space for the other food you were planning to eat which is more dense and full of starches, sugars, and calories. When you have a cleaner meal of veggies and good grains, you can eat a smaller amount of prep, however, this starts becoming a snack practice, which segues to my next point.

There's No Such Thing as a Snack

Everything you eat that requires digestion is a meal.

Stop snacking. Why? Because you're not about to be free to graze and toss some random stuff into your gut without that water-rich alkaline prep. AND the way to create and sustain that warrior-grind power is to minimize the energy that is drained through the process of digestion. If you are constantly digesting (all day long), you are using up vital energy.

Stop snacking. Why? ... If you are constantly digesting (all day long), you are using up vital energy.

Furthermore, we are preventing inflammation by keeping your meals from meeting up with each other inside your digestive system. If you eat a snack (which is actually a meal) too soon after a meal, the newly digested food may run into food that was digested from an earlier meal. That's a problem. Or if a meal is lighter and digests faster than the meal ahead of it, it's heading for a collision. Boom! Gas, bloating, acid reflux, oh my! The diagram illustrates the timing between eating meals.

A Word on Fruit

Yum! Eat it. Ignore that garbage about fruit being sugar or acidic. Raw fruit is considered alkaline, aka anti-inflammatory, just like vegetables. And for our purposes, we aren't going to have the debate that all foods with seeds are fruit. Tomatoes, avocados, bell peppers, and cucumbers, do contain seeds, but no, they are not fruit.

Here are the guidelines:

1 **Eat fruit early in the day, alone, or before any other meal.** Melon is the fruit that should always be eaten alone or with other melons because they digest much faster than any other fruit. Do not eat fruit after a non-fruit meal, unless it's been like four hours since you started digesting that previous heavy meal.

2 **Avoid meals that are a combination of fruit and non-fruit ingredients** such as apple pie, peanut butter and (fruit) jelly, cereal with bananas, or trail mix with dried fruit. Aw man! But some of those things are

A DAY OF HEALTHY EATING

wake up,
brush teeth

hydrate with at least
an additional 32 oz
throughout the day,
not at meals.

1 WATER

24-32 oz warm water
great to add lemon
or aloe vera juice

20 minutes

coffee should be enjoyed
as a snack well between
meals, black. sweetening
with maple syrup is okay.

2 BREWED WATER

tea or kombucha or
1 tablespoon apple cider
vinegar in warm water,
or coconut water

20 minutes

wait 30-60 minutes
to eat a meal after
drinking water.

3 JUICE

fresh, raw vegetable
or fruit juice

60 minutes

if you eat another meal,
wait at least 4 hours or
more (if there was a lot
of protein!) before you
eat again, and prep
with salad or raw
veggies again.

4 FRUIT & SMOOTHIES
includes green smoothies

60-120 minutes

5 WATER

30-60 minutes

alcohol should not be
consumed with meals.
as with water, consume
alcohol, then wait 30-60
minutes before food,
or even better, follow
alcohol with water, and
wait 20-60 minutes
before eating food.

6 RAW VEGGIES / SALAD

60-120 minutes

7 RAW VEGGIES / SALAD
option a cooked veggies (heavy)
option b cooked grain (heavier)
option c proteins (heaviest)
       ie. legumes, animal protein

brush teeth,
sleep well

THE TRANSITION MEAL PLAN

Not ready for A Day of Healthy Eating yet?
This daily plan is your first baby step.

wake up,
brush teeth

1   WATER

hydrate with at least
an additional 32 oz
throughout the day,
not at meals.

24-32 oz warm water
great to add lemon
or aloe vera juice

20 minutes

2   BREWED WATER

tea or kombucha or
1 tablespoon apple cider
vinegar in warm water,
or coconut water

wait 30-60 minutes
to eat a meal after
drinking water.

20 minutes

3   SALAD MEAL

large salad
with chicken.
avoid dairy and
croutons. repeat for
at least 3 meals daily.

coffee should be enjoyed
as a snack well between
meals, black. sweetening
with maple syrup is okay.

4   WATER

30-60 minutes

5   SALAD MEAL

alcohol should not be
consumed with meals.
as with water, consume
alcohol, then wait 30-60
minutes before food,
or even better, follow
alcohol with water, and
wait 20-60 minutes
before eating food.

6   WATER

30-60 minutes

7   SALAD MEAL

brush teeth,
sleep well

THE RADICAL MINOR MEAL PLAN

*Have the Transition Meal Plan down? This daily plan is
your second baby step toward A Day of Healthy Eating.*

wake up.
brush teeth

1

hydrate with at least
an additional 32 oz
throughout the day,
not at meals.

WATER

24-32 oz warm water
*great to add lemon
or aloe vera juice*

20 minutes

coffee should be enjoyed
as a snack well between
meals, black. sweetening
with maple syrup is okay.

2

BREWED WATER

tea or kombucha or
1 tablespoon apple cider
vinegar in warm water,
or coconut water

20 minutes

wait 30-60 minutes
to eat a meal after
drinking water.

3

JUICE

fresh, raw vegetable
or fruit juice

60 minutes

4

WATER

30-60 minutes

alcohol should not be
consumed with meals.
as with water, consume
alcohol, then wait 30-60
minutes before food,
or even better, follow
alcohol with water, and
wait 20-60 minutes
before eating food.

5

RAW VEGGIES / SALAD

60-120 minutes

6

RAW VEGGIES / SALAD

option a cooked veggies (heavy)
option b cooked grain (heavier)
option c proteins (heaviest)
    ie. legumes, animal protein

brush teeth.
sleep well

delicious. I agree! However, we are being radical here by preventing inflammation. Fruit is a unique type of sugar that digests super fast. So it will always cause gas and indigestion if it is mixed with items that digest slower. It will catch up to non-fruit meals that were already eaten earlier in the day.

3 Good news! This is the special exception – You CAN eat fruit mixed with the following foods: coconut, avocado, and sometimes, raw vegetables like a fruit smoothie with raw organic baby spinach. There are examples of each of these combinations in the recipe section.

Heavy Foods Last

Radical nutrition is about optimal digestion. It is the key to conserving our energy and making it possible for us to take over the world with our creativity and compassion, or to get through your day as the primary caregiver without unnecessary ass-whoopins 'cause you're so damn tired and frustrated. Whether whoopins happen in reality or in your thoughts, the energy of overwhelming frustration is toxic! These guidelines make it easier to keep your cool by keeping your body cared for!

Eating from lightest to heaviest supports this superhuman practice of preventing energy drain. What is light food and what is heavy? Let's only consider the density of the food. Fruit is the least dense and you already know you are going to eat it first.

Dried fruit and bananas are more dense than apples and strawberries. Raw veggies are lighter than cooked veggies and grains, nuts and beans

PRO TIP

Eat the denser fruit after the lighter fruit.

are heavier than cooked veggies. The heaviest, densest foods are animal fats and animal proteins. Eat these last or latest in the day because nothing else will follow them until you wake up from hours of fasting, aka sleep. That window of time gives your body the chance to digest and eliminate them completely.

Fasting

This is the most misunderstood concept in nutrition. Here's how it applies in the hustle, nutrition mentality. As I mentioned previously, the time when you are not eating is called fasting. We are all fasting every night when we go to bed until we wake up for "break" "fast". Radical nutrition teaches us that the more time we have in between meals, the more complete and uninterrupted our digestive process is. Snacking or having a meal with too little time between it and your last meal will often cause digestive issues (e.g. acid reflux, gas, bloating, fatigue, or pain). These issues are a drain on your hustle! Ain't nobody got time for that. However, giving the body longer periods of fasting allows you to experience complete digestion. And once digestion, the most labor-intensive process of your life (besides, of course, birthing children) is not happening, your body has an opportunity to use energy for other things! When your body is less taxed, it is able to address and heal disease, past and present, releasing residual stored toxins. That is why fasting can cause a lot of discomfort at times as the body involuntarily detoxes. Fasting can also create a lot of energy for handling your action plan. That source of energy is what could allow you to take that other class, or a workshop on small business or investing; and even push you to discover a new herb that helps you focus or heal a current ailment.

When your body is less taxed, it is able to address and heal disease, past and present, releasing residual stored toxins.

This is the crux of it. There's truly no limit to what humans can do with more energy and more time feeling light. Remember the religious ascetics who fasted for enlightenment? It wasn't just renunciation. They knew that a body/mind unhindered by digestion could be more focused, aware, and able to receive the secrets of life in the realm of awakening. That's us, right here, right now!

I will, however, caution that fasting should be done with knowledge and support. Fasting is not the absence of nutrition.

In this context, it is the absence of digestion. You must continue to hydrate and nourish yourself with water, tea or brewed herbs, vegetable juice, coconut water, etc., while abstaining from digesting food. I address this more in the schedule diagrams and the Liquidate Your Assets chapter. The bottom line is that the more time you have between your last meal of the night and your breakfast (which can happen at any time of the day since we now know that this term is not exclusive to a morning meal) the following day, the more opportunities you create to optimize your life force.

Mindfulness and Affirmative Food Prayer

Furthermore, I must share the power of eating meditation or mindful eating. I spent two years on silent Buddhist meditation retreats all over the country because I could not live in the world with my trauma and despair. I needed constant reinforcement of loving-kindness. At these many residential retreats I attended, we were taught that eating is a form of meditation. I learned to bring my awareness to placing the food on my plate,

We were taught that eating is a form of meditation.

craving more, chewing thoroughly, and eating up to "five bites from full". The,n I would contemplate my empty plate, or the remaining food I would be tossing out. I had dramatically improved digestion while on retreat. There is absolute science behind this – if you chew your food so thoroughly that it is liquid when you swallow, your ability to continue digesting optimally is greatly improved. For this reason, I give away my power smoothie recipes to everyone who visits my site. I include liquid meals for especially stressed food revolutionaries. Remember: Digestion is the most energy intensive process in our bodies. Whatever we can do to make it easier will give us more energy to put toward our hustle!

AND FINALLY, let's really talk about food as a healing and therapeutic experience. Praying and showing gratitude before consuming your food energizes it with love and reduces the energetic inflammation. I mentioned how animals raised for slaughter and mistreated in the process become angry food. Well, other food products, including vegetables are often cultivated in exploitative ways. The farming practices may be exploiting the earth, and/or workers are commonly paid unfairly. Imagine how that affects the vibration of the food on your table. If you've never prayed over or blessed your food before, try this food stamps prayer I wrote:

Bless all the hands that touched this food, those who grew it, those who transported it, and those who prepared it. May this food be cleansed of negativity and anger, and may we eat to sustain ourselves so that we may be forces for the transformation of suffering. May we eat to heal, taking only that which is necessary to support our energetic needs. May we give thanks for the strength we exuded to bring this food resource to our table. We give thanks to the ancestors who made it possible for us to be here today, to our descendants, and the generations that follow, who will reap the benefits of our healing.

Chapter Five

Friends with Benefits: EBT Wealth in Numbers and How to Multiply your Budget

The first date I went on in Brooklyn, after moving there from San Francisco, was at Whole Food (Stamps). This sweet, dark chocolate playwright said, "Hey, girl; go to the salad bar and get **WHATEVER** you want." She swiped that EBT card for our dinner and we gazed into each other's eyes as we dined above Union Square. Talk about romantic! I had extra kale chips 'cause I am **NOT** a cheap date.

Please don't sleep on the wealth potential of your folks with EBT cards. Not only is EBT perfectly wonderful for dating, the combination of your superfood buying force is infinite. Sometimes we need to spend a little extra during certain months to replenish our spices, or oils, or bulk products. That leaves us with less money in our daily food budget. That doesn't mean you will starve. It just means you have to get creative and social.

Potluck

Just got invited to an event and your pantry is looking slim? Take that EBT card right to the grocery store for some ingredients. You can make a salad that feeds 20 for about $10 or less. When you walk through the door with a bowl as big as a full-term baby bump, everyone will know you are an abundant manifester. Check out the salad recipes and dressings for inspiration

Got a circle of hustlers in the struggle with you? Alternate weekly potlucks that you prepare using your benefits. The host keeps the leftovers and gets bonus food for the week ahead.

Donations

Ok, so you just got laid off, but your rent payments aren't allowed to pause while you set up your (f)unemployment and land that new gig. Don't sell your food stamps - that's illegal and not very lucrative. Instead, host a vision board event, or craft-making skillshare. Provide the supplies and snacks

(all food-based), and have your homies donate for the use of space and the take-away gifts. See *Appendix C: Money-Saving Products You Can Make with Food (Stamps)* on DIY beauty and health products for ideas of what to create. At the end of the night, you should have a collection of donations to use toward your expenses, and you spent no money! Perhaps you even accepted donations for each plate of food served.

Community Supported Agriculture (CSA)

This is a type of membership in a food-buying collective that sources directly from a farmer. It's like a farmer's market VIP club. I was a member of the Central Brooklyn CSA, a project of the former New York City Coalition Against Hunger. There was a seasonal fee paid to a farmer in upstate New York. The fee was made into a sliding scale so that low-income folks could get the same amount of produce adjusted for their resources. What was even more spectacular was that if you received EBT, you didn't have to pay for the season up front. You could pay weekly. It was $8 per week for a full fruit and full vegetable share. I had SO much food I was forced to bake treats for all my friends and neighbors. I highly recommend joining your local CSA and advocating for EBT payments to be accepted if they aren't already.

Farmers Market Incentives

Almost every single farmers market I've been to in several states throughout the US accepts EBT payments for produce. A wise woman also told me this insider secret – If you go to a farm in the US, they must sell you produce or meat for half the price if you use food stamps. I've never tried it, but please let me know if it works.

Once you get to the farmers market, you will exchange your EBT credits for tokens to spend at the individual farmers stands. I always go right before the end of the market to get the better deals. Also, I rarely find a farmers market that doesn't have a bonus incentive for EBT shoppers. It is usually a matching program that doubles or triples what you would be spending (e.g. If you spend $7

with your EBT card, you will get an additional $7 to spend that day or whenever you return.). I have seen as much as triple matching.

If you are WIC-eligible, you will get farmers market vouchers during the summer. Make sure to ask for them. These vouchers can also be doubled at most markets. **OUR BABIES DESERVE IT!**

Urban Farms and Gardens

I am a huge fan of urban farms with an empowerment mission. One of my all-time favorites is City Slicker Farms in Oakland, CA. When I was dead broke, losing my affordable apartment, and healing a chronic illness, I would go to City Slicker Farms for its organic produce. The produce was offered on a sliding scale, so when I had money I paid what I could. When I had nothing, I graciously accepted free bunches of kale. Often times, these urban farms have their own CSAs and offer free bonus items weekly. I joined the CSA at the Halsey Street Garden in Brooklyn and was amazed to find them selling callaloo, aka Jamaican spinach, the best greens ever. One week, cilantro was a free bonus item. If you know Caribbean cooking you understand how valuable this is.

Food Pantries and Food Banks

I love the food bank. There is staff that manage your entire food stamps case, from start to finish, so that you don't have to waste your precious hustle force standing in line and getting frustrated over a closed case.

Secondly, I once had a YMCA job teaching culinary classes for a youth program in San Francisco's Tenderloin neighborhood. I was in charge of shopping for our program at the food bank. I was blown away by how much free food and food waste was in the ginormous warehouse. ALL the produce was free – I could have operated an underground juice bar. I actually had the YMCA invest in a good quality juicer (used from eBay) and started teaching the youth how to make green juices. It didn't stop there! One day I went to shop for ingredients and the food bank was filled to the brim with fancy Bay Area coffee beans from Blue Bottle, Ritual, etc. I filled my 1990

Volvo wagon with the bounty and taught the children how to make cold brew, French press, and pour overs. Oh those were the days! Subverting child labor restrictions creatively, in order to have little people politely serve coffee and green juice. Sigh.

In all seriousness, we need to utilize the food bank and pantries. There is a ton of food being discarded by grocery stores and bakeries that the food bank of your county is storing. A lot of it is high quality, sometimes organic, but just beyond the timeframe that a store can sell it. Not even necessarily bad! This is the same quality of food that grocery stores will put out on the curb on some evenings. I was a major patron of Perelandra Natural Food Center in Brooklyn, but mostly only on Tuesdays at 7 p.m. when they stacked crates of perfectly good food on the curb. I had friends who scheduled the Lower East Side Whole Foods' dumpster dive into their weekly agendas. They ate well, were healthy, and hosted a LOT of loft parties in WillyB...where a buffet was served and donations were accepted!

Liquidate Your Assets: The EBT of Juicing

I wrote this cookbook as a guidebook for making your food in the most efficient way so you can take care of you and yours, and not have to keep paying for more to eat. That said, our bodies become more efficient at using energy by following these principles. One of the most efficient ways to get the healing benefits of vegetables is to juice them. Doesn't juicing and juice cleanse sound expensive? It's so cool and trendy too! But in all seriousness, my father, my own first health guru, had a champion juicer at our house in the 1980s and we were making fresh apple juice all the time. Folks get down with the healthy lifestyle for sure.

PRO TIP

Take the word expensive out of your vocabulary. Harness your power as a manifestor, and start juicing for your breakthrough.

Chapter Six

Liquidate Your Assets:
The EBT of Juicing

Basic Green Juice

Green Lemonade

Cleansing Cocktail

A Word on Safety. Be gradual and gentle with juice, as you would be with any medicine, especially if you are making a big lifestyle shift. It is powerful! I have worked as a coach in the homes of some of my nutrition clients because they needed support while drinking juice in the beginning of their process. Even small amounts of a potent green juice can cause discomfort. Try small amounts of juice: four or eight ounces, to begin, and gradually begin a shift to the dietary guidelines of this cookbook. Your regimen doesn't need to be perfect because you already are! Keep in mind that therapeutic juicing probably isn't something to start while you are pregnant or breastfeeding unless there is a dire health circumstance that needs immediate attention. In that case, adjustments can be made for your safety and that of your child. I advise pregnant people and early postpartum parents to start with blended foods, aka smoothies, if they want to start a lifestyle shift. Then gradually begin having a morning juice before eating anything else during the day.

> Try small amounts of juice: four or eight ounces, to begin, and gradually begin a shift to the dietary guidelines of this cookbook.

Here are some guidelines for getting the most out of your juicing practice:

Before you get started you should know that fresh, raw juices are highly beneficial in healing current ailments, and repairing damage that may have happened in your past. The contents of your juice can be altered to address changes in your daily needs, and as you get more familiar with your body, you will begin to notice which juice combination works best for you. For instance, if you have a hangover, you may have more cucumbers; or if you're constipated, you may add more beets.

By the way, juices are not smoothies. This is a huge misnomer I hear about a lot. Let me demystify it. Juices are straight liquids with all the pulp extracted. This means there is no digestion involved. Straight medicine. Smoothies are **MEALS** that you **MUST** digest, even though they are in liquid form. They are blended from whole fruits, vegetables, and "milks" or water.

1 **Get a juicer.** Juicers can be pricey, but there are definitely affordable ones. Check out sites like Amazon, eBay, and Craigslist for used models. If you already own a high power blender like the VitaMix, you can blend vegetables and then strain the juice through a nut milk bag. I hella do not vouch for this method because it is messy, but you gotta do what you gotta do if you are on a tight budget. If you're super broke and need immediate juice, cop a goodwill device and start saving for your upgrade. My homie had a Hamilton Beach juicer. It had to be held together with rubber bands to work. She got it at the flea market for $5 thinking it was a humidifier. It saved me hella dough when I was visiting her from out of town, and had already become accustomed to daily juicing. Some excellent juicers can be found at www. discountjuicers.com. I recommend the Lequip, Breville, and Omega.

2 **Make your juice part of your morning ritual.** Have juice on an empty stomach with plenty of time before your first solid meal. This allows your system to absorb the nutrients maximally. Wait 30-60 minutes after drinking juice before eating.

3 **Juice the good stuff.** Emphasize your morning juice as your **special healing blend**. Include plenty of dark leafy greens, alkalizing elements like lemon, and digestive support like cabbage and ginger.

4 **Drink up!** Have at least **16-32 ounces** if you can. While spinach, kale, and parsley produce a small liquid volume when juiced, celery, cabbage, and cucumber greatly increase your total volume.

5 **Locate affordable juice bars.** A local juice bar is ideal for the days you want to skip the juicing and cleanup. Jamba Juice does not count! However, Groupon deals on juice cleanses that can be shipped to your house is a perfect option.

Basic Green Juice

(makes 32 oz, approximate cost: $5)

Depending on your juicer, you may need to sequence your ingredients in a way that supports optimal liquid extraction. Using an Omega Masticating Juicer, I tend to juice in order of the recipe. Centrifugal juicers sometimes work best when mixing leafy veggies with stalkier produce.

Here are the underlying principles of creating a radical juice:

1   **Juice at least a bunch of greens** (if running tight on budget, try some cheap parsley). This will not produce a lot of juice, probably 2-6 ounces and will be bitter and potent.

2   Next, **increase your volume with water-rich elements such as cucumbers**, usually several for under a dollar, and celery. Fennel is a great enhancer for a bit of spice and digestive alkalizing,and creates a lot of liquid volume when juiced. I get a couple fennel bulbs for around $2.

3   As with all produce, prices will change, and you may need more or less of something depending on the size of each item. I give suggested prices as a guideline and to illuminate the affordability of juice as medicine. It may not be something you can do every day of the month, however, as a

PRO TIP

I use carrots to clear a block of fruit pulp mush in the masticating juicer.

therapeutic treatment for temporary and longer lasting dis-ease, it is more affordable than a trip to a hospital or prescription medication.

These are the only two recipes I will give in this book because they are the most cost-effective way to use your resources:

Green Lemonade
(makes 32 oz)

	Cost	Notes
1 bunch spinach or other leafy green	$2	whichever is on sale, organic when possible or on the "Clean Fifteen" list
1-2 cucumbers	$1	
3 celery stalks	$0.50	
1 fennel bulb	$1	
1 lemon	$0.30	
1 inch fresh ginger	$0.25	
2 apples	$1	(optional for flavor, organic when possible. Granny Smith are my favorite for light sweetness, other varieties will give a sweeter flavor)

Enhancers I Love

Pineapple
Just a few fresh peeled chunks will electrify the flavor of your juice!

Strawberries
Just a couple berries give any juice a cheery bright taste and appeals greatly to children.

Garlic
If you seriously want to address acute illness and emit a spicy odor through your pores. Use sparingly!

Ginger
No need to peel.

Cleansing Cocktail
(makes 32 oz)

	Cost	Notes
1 bunch spinach or other leafy green	< $2	purchase whichever is on sale, organic when possible
1-2 cucumbers	$1	
1 fennel bulb	$1	
1 lb carrots		
1/2 beet or 1 small beet	$0.50	
1 in fresh ginger	$0.25	
2 apples	$1	optional for flavor

Lemon
Keep the peel on if organic, remove if conventional.

Grapes
Just a few make it super sweet.

Lime
Per lemon recommendations and as a substitute for lemon.

Substitute accordingly for your taste preferences.

As always, substitute accordingly for your taste preferences. To be totally real, there are times when my fridge is missing certain items for green juice and I wind up making hybrids like a mostly green juice with two pounds of carrots for increasing liquid volume if I'm out of apples or cucumbers (remember, the leafy greens are the source of concentrated nutrients, while the other fruits and veggies expand the liquid volume and enhance the flavor). The most important thing to remember is to juice as frequently as possible!

How can you do a radical juice cleanse or an increased detox experience? It's simpler than it sounds. Your body, the gorgeous abundant magnetic temple that it is, has a simple equation for detoxing. To cleanse the body, you simply increase the length of fasting time in your day. Use juices to extend that time since they will supply vital nutrients and energy to keep you going without slowing down to digest food. Seek support from veteran juicers before taking on long periods of fasting.

Ideally, you are fasting twelve hours minimum, give or take, because your last meal was around 8 p.m. and you won't eat breakfast until 8 a.m. or so. You can extend any fasting period by an hour or two if you have a juice first, after morning hydration. Your digestion will be optimized for eating food next, preferably fruit because it is light, and you will have more time to release and complete the digestion from the day before.

Ideally, you are fasting twelve hours minimum.

Here's a diagram for a day of gentle juice fasting.

RECOMMENDED READING

Walker, Norman. *Fresh Vegetable and Fruit Juices.*
Norwalk Press

A DAY OF GENTLE JUICE FASTING

wake up,
brush teeth

1 WATER
tea or herbs
or kombucha
or apple cider
vinegar (ACV)
in water

2 COCONUT WATER

3 VEGETABLE JUICE
every 1-2 hours

4 TEA/BLACK COFFEE
as snacks

5 WATER,
WATER,
WATER

6 SALAD MEAL
for gentle approach

brush teeth.
sleep well

Chapter Seven

Blendefits: The Essential Smoothies

Blended foods, aka smoothies, offer a number of benefits for healing and lifestyle rejuvenation. Especially if you are on the go, a smoothie or liquid meal can save precious minutes by decreasing time spent eating. While saving time is important, blended foods offer the added bonus of being easier to assimilate in the body. Once food is processed in a blender or food processor the initial mastication stage has already been completed. Your digestive system has less work to do to access the nutrients in your food. Since some of y'all are re-learning to chew food thoroughly, the blending technique ensures that what we consume has

Your digestive system has less work to do to access the nutrients in your food.

been reduced to the smallest possible size before entering the stomach. Blended meals are also an option for eating light when there is a reason to be concerned about healthy elimination and colon function. They are a healthy medium between complete juice fasting and eating well-combined and timely-spaced solid foods.

Step 1: What to have on hand

Coconut milk or Coconut water

I strongly discourage dairy, soy, nut, and grain milks. If you use coconut you avoid making a difficult combination to digest, and coconut combines well with fruit, unlike grain and nut milks, which are derived from more complex fats and starches. When buying coconut products look for the coconut milk beverage in glass bottles in the juice section (this is usually a mixture of coconut and white grape juice which costs $4-6/bottle), or the half-gallon cartons of coconut milk in the refrigerated section (So Delicious or Silk costs about $4). There are also non-refrigerated quarts available at Trader Joe's and Whole Foods on the soy and grain milk shelves ($2). Your coconut water should be natural and unsweetened. Trader Joe's liters cost about $3, and many other stores carry liters for about $4-6.

Fresh Squeezed Fruit Juice

Another option for blending smoothies is to use fresh juice from your juicer. Apple is simple. Be sure to avoid using melon juices as melon should be eaten alone per Ayurvedic rules and because it digests faster than any fruit.

Avocado

Avocados whip up decadently in a smoothie. I recommend them over bananas for adding creaminess to your beverage. They pick up the taste of the rest of the contents of the smoothie or blended meal without adding extra sugar. And you just can't get enough avocado in your diet.

Fresh Fruit

Any local seasonal fruit that is low in pesticides or organic.

Frozen Fruit

Frozen organic berries tend to be cheaper than fresh ones. Check out the freezer section of your local market for organic strawberries and blueberries (both high in pesticides if eaten conventionally), or head to TJs for freezer packs around $2.

Blender or Food Processor

Of course a high speed blender like VitaMix, Blendtec, Breville, and even Ninja offer the best blending capabilities, however, any conventional blender or food processor will get the job done. The Magic Bullet is a high-speed blender as well.

PRO TIP

Increase the volume of any smoothie by adding water (or your preferred affordable blending juices and milks) and more sweetener. The smoothie will be thinner after being extended, but it will still be delicious.

Each of these recipes makes a large smoothie meal 20-40 or so ounces, that can be shared among 2-3 people, or stored for a couple of days in the fridge. Use plain water or ice instead of coconut milk if your funds are low. The smoothies still taste pretty good that way. Also, if you are vegan, use maple syrup or another sweetener you love, instead of honey.

Ginger Berry O

1-2 inches peeled fresh ginger

$^1/_4$-$^1/_2$ cup fresh or frozen berries

$^1/_2$-1 whole Hass avocado or $^1/_2$ Florida avocado

8-12 ounces coconut milk or water

honey to taste

pinch of sea salt

juice of $^1/_2$ lime or lemon

ice or water for consistency

directions
Blend to desired consistency. Best as a thinner rather than a creamier smoothie, so experiment with the amount of avocado and liquid.

Strawberry Cardamogasm O

1-2 handfuls frozen strawberries

$^1/_2$-1 whole Hass avocado or $^1/_2$ Florida avocado

8-12 ounces coconut milk

$^1/_4$ teaspoon cardamom

pinch of sea salt

$^1/_2$ teaspoon vanilla extract or powdered vanilla

honey or maple syrup to taste

juice of $^1/_2$ lemon, optional (for added boost)

water or ice for consistency

directions
Blend until creamy.

Mango Lassi

1/2-1 mango, peeled and deseeded

coconut meat or 1/2 Florida avocado

8-12 ounces coconut milk

1-2 tablespoons rose water

pinch of sea salt

honey to taste

ice or water for consistency

directions
Blend until creamy.

Coconut Horchata

12 ounces coconut milk

1/4 - 1/2 teaspoon cinnamon

optional spices, add to taste (cardamom, cloves)

ice

maple syrup, to taste

directions
Can be blended or shaken in a jar.

Almond Joy

This is lovely as a slushy, creamy frozen treat.

1/2 Florida avocado

16-20 ounces coconut milk

2 pitted dates

pinch of sea salt

1/2 teaspoon almond extract

cinnamon, to taste

maple syrup, to taste

ice

directions
Blend until creamy.

Avocolada

1/2-1 whole Hass avocado or
1/2 Florida avocado

8-12 ounces coconut milk

pinch of sea salt

juice of 1/2 lime

honey, to taste

ice, optional

directions
Blend until silky.

Tropical Dreamsicle

juice of 2 tangerines

1/2 Hass avocado or 1/4 Florida avocado

1/4 cup frozen pineapple

10 ounces coconut water or milk

1 teaspoon vanilla

honey, to taste

pinch of salt

directions
Blend until creamy.

Black Raspberry

12-20 ounces coconut milk or water, or plain water

1/2 Hass avocado

1/2 cup raspberries/ strawberries

1-2 tablespoons cacao or cocoa powder unsweetened

1/2 teaspoon vanilla (alcohol

free, if possible)

honey, to taste

pinch of sea salt

ice

directions
Blend until creamy.

Peanut Butter Jelly Time

This is the essence of the peanut butter and jelly sandwich but without gluten grains, funky trans fat peanut butter, and processed sugar.

12-20 ounces coconut milk or coconut water

1 banana and/or $^1/_2$ avocado (any kind)

1-2 cups frozen strawberries

1 tablespoon sunflower seed butter

maple syrup, to taste

directions
Blend until smooth.

Peanut Punch

12-20 ounces coconut milk

1 banana and/or $^1/_2$ avocado (any kind)

1 tablespoon sunflower seed butter

scoop of Irish moss jelly, optional

maple syrup, to taste

directions
Blend until smooth.

Sweet Blueberry Vanilla

12-16 ounces coconut milk or water

fresh coconut meat, optional

1 banana and/or $^1/_2$ avocado

2 cups frozen blueberries (organic when possible)

$^1/_2$ tablespoon vanilla extract

maple syrup, to taste

directions
Blend until smooth.

Acai Smoothie or Bowl

Smoothie: 16 ounces desired liquid
Smoothie Bowl: 8 ounces (or less) desired liquid

1-2 cups frozen berries

1/2 cup frozen mango

1 banana

1/2 avocado

2 teaspoons acai powder or 1 unsweetened acai packet

(about $.50 - $1)

maple syrup or honey, to taste

directions
Blend gradually increasing speed.

Cacao to Cacao

I use this when I need a mood and energy boost!

12-16 ounces coconut milk

2 cups frozen red berries

1/2 avocado

fresh coconut meat, optional

1-2 tablespoons cacao powder

2 teaspoons vanilla extract

maple syrup, to taste

directions
Blend until smooth.

PRO TIP

Make any of these recipes a green smoothie by adding two handfuls of raw organic baby spinach leaves. Baby spinach is way cheaper than green powder, and it is EBT eligible!

Make fruit a meal! Remember to eat fruit alone and allow plenty of time between your next foods. Since it digests and moves quickly, here are some options for making a big and satisfying fruit meal.

Smoothie Bowls

Take any smoothie above and reduce the liquid by half so that it is thicker. Pour into a bowl. Top with any dried fruit, fresh berries, coconut, avocado chunks, pomegranate seeds, or banana slices. Avoid nuts and granola to make a cleaner combination that is simpler to digest.

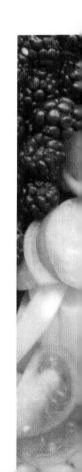

FROM SMOOTHIE TO BOWL

try converting these recipes!

Strawberry Cardamogasm
Avocolada
Tropical Dreamsicle
Acai Smoothie

suggested toppings:

shredded coconut
seeds of any type (chia, hemp)
chopped fresh fruit

Citrus and Avocado Salad

1 grapefruit and/or several
seasonal citrus fruits (orange,
Satsuma, tangerine, etc.)

1 avocado

sprinkle of coconut flakes

directions
Peel and chop the citrus
into bite-size chunks. Split
avocado, remove seed, slice
into chunks and scoop out
onto citrus. Decorate with
coconut flakes.

Peaches, Apples, and Coconut with Honey

mix of seasonal stone fruit
(peaches, nectarines) and
apples

fresh coconut meat or
coconut flakes

avocado chunks, optional

directions
Chop fruit, removing any
seeds or pits. Add coconut or
avocado chunks and flakes.
Drizzle with honey.

Chapter Eight

Roughage: From Margins to Center
(Salads and Meal Preps)

salads

Basic Mix

People Dem Want Roots Salad

By Any Greens Necessary

Blasian Salad

Ensalada Califas

Sweet Cilantro Lime Salad

Uptown Julie Brown's Kale
Salad and Kale Chips

Carrot Coconut Slaw

Jerk Coleslaw

Oakland Scavenger Salad

liquid salads

Tomato Basil

Red Soup

Cucumber Gazpacho

dressings, sauces, and Pâtés

Simple Oil and Lemon Juice

Creamy Sesame Ginger

Lemon Tahini Dressing Base

Creamy Cilantro

Simple Sesame Ginger

Un-peanut Sauce

Versatile Pesto

Cashew Cheese Sauce
and Dressing

Curry Almond

Smoky Sun Dried Tomato
Sunflower Seed Pâté

Curry Sunflower Seed Pâté

fun raw veggie meals

Avocado Dip with
Sliced Veggies

Nori Hand Rolls

Lettuce, Cabbage,
or Kale Rolls

Cauliflower Ceviche

Rice Paper Spring Rolls

The key to success with food stamps is to understand how to maximize the amount of food you can eat. Roughage (raw leafy greens) is relatively cheap and substantially bulky. This means you can spend just a little bit of money and create a huge dish that not only fills you up, but also provides great health benefits.

When you include a large amount of roughage in your diet, you reap the benefits of eating raw foods. If you are having large salads twice a day, you are eating at least 50% raw. The benefits of raw veggies are infinite because they alleviate digestion fatigue and clear out stagnant, inflammation-prone blockages. Filling up on salad crowds out the space in your stomach for heavier foods. If you have a weight-loss goal, this is an effective way to dramatically reduce calories. Furthermore, the salad, which is water-rich and alkaline, serves to prep your digestive tract for your heavier food choices. That means more efficient digestion, and more energy for you to do what you do best – shine as a beneficial presence on the planet!

If you are having large salads twice a day, you are eating at least 50% raw.

The benefits of raw veggies are infinite.

Here's a new perspective – Salad is not a side dish, a garnish, or a small plate that precedes the main course. In this practice of eating, salad becomes a large main course around which other cooked or dense foods are planned. When you think large, think about the size of a salad that a family of three can share for dinner, or the amount of leafy greens in one pre-washed salad mix in a bag. This is the amount that one person should eat for a meal or as a meal prep. Salad is so much more than a bowl of greens. In this chapter, we make tasty masterpieces that are equally appealing to the eyes.

Here are some fun ways to eat raw veggies:

Carrot and beet ribbons

Using a veggie peeler, remove and discard outer skin. Continue peeling long ribbons into the salad.

Cucumber noodles

Using the same strategy from the carrot and beet ribbons, peel a cucumber into flat noodles. These noodles can also be used as raw pasta.

Fetti (In honor of Mac Mall)

Grate carrots and beets into colorful sprinkles.

Massaged kale

Wash and de-stem kale leaves of any variety. Tear or cut into bite-size pieces. Toss with lemon juice, salt, and olive oil to coat. Knead and caress until coated. Let sit. Eat alone or add to your salad recipe.

Bacon bits aka sundried tomatoes

Chop tomatoes into fine strips or soak in hot water for a few minutes, and then chop for a softer texture. I threw these in a salad that I made and shared with a carnivorous friend who thought the chewy salty surprises scattered about the leaves were meat!

Avocado

Cut into small chunks. Such a delicate pale green, such an incredible buttery flavor, such a rich texture.

Jicama chunks

Peel a jicama and cut half into small cubes. Cut the other half into sticks for a quick digestion prep before eating a snack.

Seasoned Juicer Pulp

Use the carrot/celery/greens/cucumber/beet pulp from your juice. Toss with ANY dressing option and store in the fridge. Use a scoop for a quick salad topping or use as stuffing in patties or rice buns.

Toppings

Raw nuts or seeds (almond, pumpkin, sesame, cashew, walnut, sunflower), raw or toasted nori (seaweed wrapper), Sauerkraut or kimchee, fancy greens and herbs (frisee, watercress, purslane, cilantro, basil), chopped or pressed garlic, grated ginger, chopped scallions, sliced fennel, sliced radish, chopped red pepper, finely sliced celery, olives, or pickled veggies.

Basic Mix
(makes about two big salads)

Since salad is such a big part of our dietary intake, it's important to have the ingredients for making a basic mix on hand at all times. This base is colorful and enticing, and will remind you of how creative you can be with your veggies. I find this salad is good to go on its own, but gets more and more fabulous with all the recipe remixes that follow.

1 romaine heart or 6 romaine leaves

1/4 green or red cabbage

1 small red or yellow onion, diced

1 cucumber, chopped into bite-size slices (peeled, if conventional)

2 Roma tomatoes, chopped or

2 handfuls grape tomatoes

squirt of fresh lemon

directions
Combine all ingredients in a large bowl. Toss with a squirt of fresh lemon juice to keep fresh.

People Dem Want Roots Salad

basic mix

1 small beet, shredded or peeled into ribbons

1 carrot, shredded or peeled into ribbons

handful of raw cashew pieces

directions
Fill your salad bowl halfway with Basic Mix. Shred or peel your carrot and beet root veggies onto the Basic Mix.

Toss with Curry Almond dressing and sprinkle with cashew pieces.

By Any Greens Necessary

(Dedicated to Tracye Lynn McQuirter)

basic mix

2 handfuls baby spinach leaves

1 handful massaged kale

small bunch frisee

cubes from one avocado

kale chip croutons (see Uptown Julie Brown's Kale Chip recipe)

directions

Start with filling your large salad bowl halfway with Basic Mix. Add additional fancy greens. Toss with avocado cubes until slightly coated with avocado. Top with kale chips as croutons. I save the last crumbs from the kale chip bag when I buy store bought kale chips to use on top of salads. Toss with Creamy Cilantro dressing.

Blasian Salad

basic mix

2 sheets shredded nori

1 handful basil leaves, chopped

2 scallions, chopped

1 handful walnuts

$1/_2$ an avocado

1 tablespoon grated ginger

dash of sesame and toasted sesame oil

$1/_4$ teaspoon chili garlic sauce or hot sauce

directions

Toss until avocado gets creamy.

Ensalada Califas

(Does not use Basic Mix)

2 hearts of romaine or 1 romaine head, chopped

$^1/_2$-1 red pepper

1 handful cilantro leaves

1 medium onion, chopped

2 celery stalks, sliced finely

2 tomatillos, chopped

sprinkle of sea salt

fresh juice of $^1/_2$ lemon

1 large ripe avocado, chopped

radish slices for garnish

directions
Toss all ingredients and mix until avocado becomes creamy and less chunky (alternately, mash avocado with lemon juice and add to salad after tossed). Serve with radish garnish.

You can optionally add a tablespoon of cold-pressed grapeseed oil for more essential fatty acids (EFAs) if desired.

Sweet Cilantro Lime Salad

$^1/_2$ head red cabbage, shredded

$^1/_2$ head green cabbage, shredded

$^1/_2$ lb. carrots, grated

1 avocado

1 bunch cilantro, destemmed

1 tablespoon coconut sugar

juice of 2 limes

salt, to taste

drizzle of toasted sesame oil

directions
Add cabbage and carrots to large bowl. Blend avocado with cilantro, lime juice, salt, and sesame oil. Drizzle over salad and toss.

Uptown Julie Brown's Kale Salad

Cheese Sauce

1 cup soaked Brazil nuts
or cashews (sub sunflower
seeds or avocado for allergy
concerns)

1 red bell pepper

3 teaspoons turmeric

2 cloves garlic

juice of 1 lemon

$1/2$ teaspoon sea salt

directions

Combine all ingredients in
food processor and blend until
thoroughly combined and
almost creamy.

Massaged Kale

3 bunches of kale

3 avocados

3 tomatoes

2 cucumbers

1 white onions

2 sheets of nori

1 lemons

drizzle of olive oil

dulse powder, optional

directions

Wash and de-stem kale. Stack
leaves and roll into a bunch.
Cut strips by slicing the roll
to create a chiffonade. Place
strips in bowl and massage
with lemon juice and olive oil.
Cover and let kale marinate.
Add chopped tomatoes,
cucumbers, avocado, onion,
shredded nori, and dulse
powder. Toss with sauce.
Keeps well for a few days in
the fridge!

Kale Chips

2 bunches of curly kale,
destemmed, cut into 1 inch
pieces

$1/2$ cup cheese sauce, nut or
seed based

directions

Toss kale pieces with cheese
sauce. Spread coated kale on
parchment paper atop a

baking sheet. Bake for
20 minutes in the lowest
temperature your oven uses or
180°F. Remove and check for
dryness. Return to the oven
to bake longer, if necessary.
Serve alone or as salad garnish
and croutons. Alternatively,
kale chips do even better when
made in a dehydrator instead
of the oven.

Carrot Coconut Slaw

4 carrots, grated

2-4 radishes, sliced thinly

$^1/_2$ cabbage, grated (Green is good; red is fancy!)

1 fennel bulb, grated

juice of 1 lime

$^1/_2$ teaspoon cumin

1 teaspoon salt

$^1/_4$ cup sunflower oil

$^1/_2$ cup toasted coconut flakes (simple dried flakes are fine too

directions
Add all grated ingredients to a large bowl. Mix lime juice, salt, cumin, and sunflower oil in a separate bowl or shaking jar. Pour oil mixture over grated veggies and toss. Sprinkle with coconut when serving, or mix all coconut flakes into the slaw, if you prefer. Serve as a salad or the topping of a larger salad.

Jerk Coleslaw

1 cabbage, shredded

1 red cabbage, shredded

3 large carrots, grated

1 cup walnuts, optional

1 tablespoon Jerk Seasoning (*Chapter Thirteen - Essential Spices, Blends, and Easy Hacks*)

$^1/_4$ cup vegan mayo

juice of 1-2 limes

water

directions
Combine jerk seasoning with mayo, and whisk. Add water and lime for to adjust consistency. Dress salad with mayo sauce and toss thoroughly. Add walnuts and mix well.

Oakland Scavenger Salad

by Anita de Asis aka The Lumpia Lady

There's so much abundance in Oakland! Make this recipe when it is the end of the month and your food stamps are almost gone! We all know that time of the month! All you need to use your food stamps for is the olive oil and seasonings for the dressings. Look for the nature spots in your area. And please note: Most things called weeds that grow plentifully are medicinal foods.

1. **Head for the hills and harvest!** Joaquin Miller Park or Tilden Park in the Bay Area: shepherd's purse, mint, blackberries, dandelion greens - Lightly steam so they are edible.

2. **Walk around your neighborhood -** Any fruit trees that are hanging onto the sidewalk area are no longer considered part of the tree owner's property and you are legally protected to pick the fruit hanging/growing on sidewalks. This goes for landscaped area, as well. Recently, cities have been using decorative lettuce and cabbages as landscapes. Don't be greedy! Take only what you need!

3. **Talk to people in the neighborhood who have gardens.** See if you can have their surplus fruit. Fruit trees usually produce WAY more than one family can eat, and it is my experience that even when I ask complete strangers if I can harvest some of their excess fruit, they are happy to share. Excess fruit usually is wasted, and you save them a mega fallen-fruit cleanup. And to promote reciprocity and neighborly love, you could always offer a barter or trade (I offer hand made jewelry or yard work.).

4. **If you have a community garden in your city** find out if it's open to the public to harvest. Here in Oakland, most are not. But in West Oakland, People's Grocery has an abundant garden that anyone is welcome to take from, as needed.

directions

Chop, slice, dice your harvest findings. Toss them all together.

Dressing 1

If you found citrus fruits, juice them. Add olive oil and salt and pepper, to taste.

Dressing 2

If you harvested some avocados, smash them. Add lemon juice, olive oil, salt, pepper, and a little chili, to taste. Stir into a liquid consistency.

Dressing 3

If you harvested lots of herbs, mix equal amounts of olive oil and the vinegar of your choice, salt, and pepper. Add a little honey and minced garlic, to taste. Stir and simmer for about 5 minutes. Allow the dressing to cool off before you use it. Shake or stir well before dressing your salad.

Make these savory smoothies to have before a heavier meal without having to spend all that time and energy eating a whole salad.

Tomato Basil

1 romaine heart

2 roma tomatoes

1 avocado

1 handful fresh basil leaves

1 tablespoon nutritional yeast

1 tablespoon olive oil

juice of ¹/₂ lemon

salt and pepper, to taste

directions
Blend thoroughly.

Red Soup

1 romaine heart

2 large tomatoes

1 large red bell pepper

¹/₂ avocado

¹/₄ cup raw sunflower seeds

1 tablespoon nutritional yeast

juice of ¹/₂ lime

salt and pepper, to taste

directions
Blend thoroughly.

Cucumber Gazpacho

1 cup organic baby spinach leaves

1 cucumber, chopped into small cubes, set aside

1 cucumber for blending or use 1 cup water

1 avocado

1 celery stalk

1 tablespoon nutritional yeast

juice of 1 lemon

1 tablespoon olive oil

$^1/_2$ teaspoon sea salt

$^1/_4$ fresh fennel bulb

$^1/_4$ cup fresh dill, optional

directions
Set cucumber chunks aside. Blend all ingredients until smooth. Add cucumber chunks to blended soup.

Glamming Up Your Salad

You are encouraged to dress your salad with the simplest dressings possible. The store-bought dressings are often mixed with questionable oils, dairy products, or vinegars. What do I have against vinegar? Just that I want to prevent gassy fermentation in your tummy. Keep raw apple cider vinegar on hand for your morning routine, fasting, or illness. Use white vinegar for cleaning. Avoid vinegar in preserved and pickled products, too. The following recipes are options for simple delicious enhancements that maintain the benefits of your raw veggies.

Basics to have on hand for creating salad dressings: Lemons and limes, fresh ginger and garlic, tahini (raw, unhulled is best and generally costs $10/jar. Hulled costs about $5.), raw almond butter (High-end brands are about $12/jar. Trader Joe's brand is $5.), wheat-free tamari or soy sauce, Bragg's liquid amino acids or coconut amino acids, good quality cold-pressed oils of olive, grapeseed, sesame, toasted sesame, salt, and peppers.

Simple Oil and Lemon Juice

$^1/_4$ cup olive or grapeseed oil

juice of 1-2 lemons

2 garlic cloves, pressed

salt and pepper, to taste

directions
Combine in a bowl and whisk. Add all ingredients to a jar and shake. *Jar method allows you to mix a grip of it and store for future use.*

Creamy Sesame Ginger

1 tablespoon tahini

1 tablespoon sesame oil

$^1/_2$ teaspoon toasted sesame oil

1 teaspoon tamari

1 tablespoon fresh ginger

$^1/_2$ cup water (additional water for consistency

directions
Add all ingredients except oil to food processor. Slowly add oil as you blend. *Use water to make a thinner dressing.*

Lemon Tahini Dressing Base

1 cup water

2 tablespoons tahini

1 tablespoon maple syrup or honey (non-vegan version)

juice of 1 lemon

salt, to taste

directions
Combine in a blender or food processor and blend until tahini is completely liquefied in the water.

Creamy Cilantro

2 tablespoons almond butter

$^1/_2$ cup water (add additional water for consistency)

juice of $^1/_2$ lemon

2 handfuls cilantro leaves

$^1/_2$ teaspoon salt

2 tablespoons olive or grapeseed oil

directions
Place almond butter in blender or food processor and pulse lightly. Slowly add water until the almond butter is liquified. Add all remaining ingredients, saving the oil to be added last while mixture is processing

Simple Sesame Ginger

$^1/_2$ cup sesame oil

2 tablespoons soy aminos/tamari

2 teaspoons toasted sesame oil

1 tablespoon fresh ginger, shredded

directions
Add all ingredients to a jar and shake.

Un-Peanut Sauce

Great for the rice paper wraps, or just add more water to make a salad dressing!

2 tablespoons sunbutter

1-2 teaspoons sriracha or chili sauce, optional

1 teaspoon grated ginger, optional

1 tablespoon maple syrup

1 tablespoon vegan mayo, optional

1 teaspoon tamari

1 cup water

juice of $^1/_2$ lime

directions
Blend ingredients. Taste and add more of any ingredient until you love this versatile sauce.

Versatile Pesto

While basil leaves are most familiar, this recipe can also be used with radish leaves, arugula, spinach, or kale.

2 handfuls fresh basil leaves, destemmed

1/4 olive oil

1 tablespoon almond butter (or 1/4 cup pine nuts or cheaper option)

1 tablespoon nutritional yeast

2 garlic cloves

1/2 teaspoon sea salt

1/4 teaspoon ground pepper

1/4 teaspoon smoked paprika, optional

juice of 1 lemon

directions
Combine in blender or food processor. Great coating for kale chips!

Cashew Cheese Sauce and Dressing

1 cup cashews

1/2 lemon

1-2 tablespoon nutritional yeast

1-2 garlic cloves

2 tablespoon olive oil

1 teaspoon salt

1/2 teaspoon black pepper

1/2 cup fresh water for creating consistency

directions
Soak cashews in water for twenty minutes minimum. Drain water. Add soaked cashews and all other ingredients to blender. Blend while adding water until desired consistency is reached. Use a thicker cheese for spreads and to put in tamales. Use a medium consistency for pasta (It's totally alfredo sauce!). Use a thin consistency for salad dressings.

Curry Almond

1 tablespoon almond butter

1 teaspoon curry powder

2 teaspoons honey

$^{1}/_{2}$ cup water, almond, or coconut milk

$^{1}/_{2}$ teaspoon salt

additional salt and water for making a larger volume

directions
Combine all ingredients and blend.

Smoky Sun Dried Tomato Sunflower Seed Pâté

1 cup sunflower seeds, soaked

$^{1}/_{4}$ cup sun-dried tomatoes

1 tablespoon nutritional yeast, optional

1 tablespoon olive oil

$^{1}/_{2}$ teaspoon sea salt

$^{1}/_{4}$ teaspoon ground white

pepper

1 teaspoon liquid smoke

water to adjust consistency

directions
Blend all ingredients until you create a stiff paste. Add water to reach the consistency you prefer.

Curry Sunflower Seed Pâté

1 cup sunflower seeds, soaked

2 teaspoons curry powder

1 tablespoon nutritional yeast, optional

1 tablespoon olive oil

$^{1}/_{2}$ teaspoon sea salt

$^{1}/_{4}$ teaspoon ground white pepper

water (to adjust consistency

directions
Blend all ingredients until you create a stiff paste. Add water to reach the consistency you prefer.

Make these savory smoothies to have before a heavier meal without having to spend all that time and energy eating a whole.

Avocado Dip with Sliced Veggies

2 ripe avocados

1 red bell pepper

1 large carrot

1 stick of celery

1 cucumber

2 teaspoons nut or seed parmesan

directions
Remove seeds and scoop avocados out of their skins and into a large bowl. Mash with a fork until a thick mixture chunky paste. Sprinkle with parmesan (parm) and stir until you reach your desired consistency.

Make veggie slices out of the remaining ingredients and dip! This avocado dip is also a favorite for spreading on warm Manna bread or toast.

Nori Hand Rolls

Nori Sheets

directions
Make any salad recipe. Cut nori sheet into quarters. Holding a nori square in the palm of your hand, spoon about a quarter cup of salad onto the center. Roll the nori up like a cone around the salad, and voila...hand roll!

Lettuce, Cabbage, or Kale Rolls

This fun meal calls for any kind of big leaves you can find. My favorites are romaine lettuce, red cabbage, Napa cabbage, rainbow chard, and massaged or blanched kale or collard leaves.

For thicker leaves, like lacinato kale or collard greens, use this quick blanching process to soften.

Blanching Process
Bring water to boil in a large stock pot. Once boiling, use tongs to immerse clean leaves in the water. Allow to boil for 30 seconds to a minute, then remove from water with tongs, and cool in an ice bath.

directions
Start with leaves flat on a plate. Add a small amount of any salad to the center of the widest end of the leaf. Spread any pâté on top of the salad and along the center on the leaf toward the smaller end. Roll leaf from the wider end toward the smaller end and use pâté to seal if necessary.

Cauliflower Ceviche
by Marlene Sanchez

1 bag of diced cauliflower or
1/2 head of cauliflower, diced

10 limes

1 red onion, diced

3 tomatoes, diced

1 bunch cilantro, destemmed, chopped finely

4 avocados, sliced

1/2 teaspoon sea salt

bag of tostadas, optional

directions
Add cauliflower and onion to a large bowl with lime juice and a couple pinches of salt. Let sit for at least 20 minutes or until cauliflower is soft. Add tomato and cilantro. Add additional salt to taste. Serve on tostadas, tacos, or add to a salad.

Rice Paper Spring Rolls

tapioca-based round rice paper

veggie sticks

whole romaine lettuce leaves

mint leaves

cilantro

lime wedges

nut or seed pâté, optional

Un-peanut sauce (*Chapter Eight - Roughage*)

large bowl with warm water

directions
Gather your favorite ingredients. Typically a salad recipe is too wet for success with this method. Use larger veggie pieces like sliced cucumber, carrot, jicama, and avocado.

Immerse one rice paper into a bowl of warm water for 10-15 seconds. Remove from water, and place rice paper on a plate or work surface. Place a medium-sized romaine leaf or multiple small leaves of romaine in the center of the wrap to act like a bowl for the other ingredients. Place a few veggie sticks and avocado on the romaine. Add your choice of mint or cilantro. Squeeze a few drops of lime. Roll like a burrito by folding in the shorter ends, then rolling lengthwise, enclosing the romaine leaf and its contents.

It's optional to add some nut or seed pâté before rolling, as the typical recipe includes shrimp or tofu.

Chapter Nine

Cooked Vegetables:
Heavier than Raw Veggies

Butternut Curry

This is a quick and super simple recipe for using your abundance of seasonal squash.

1 butternut squash

1 can coconut milk

1 tablespoon curry powder

1 teaspoon garam masala

$^1/_4$ teaspoon sea salt

water or vegetable broth for consistency

directions
Peel the squash and remove the seeds. Cut into 2 inch chunks. Steam until soft. Add squash and remaining ingredients to blender, reserving the water (or vegetable broth) to pour slowly into the mixture while processing until desired consistency is reached.

Cauliflower Soup and Mashed Potatoes

Three ways to make a meal out of 1 cauliflower!

1 head of cauliflower

1 tablespoon nutritional yeast

1 tablespoon olive oil

juice of $^1/_2$ lemon

1 clove fresh garlic or $^1/_2$ teaspoon garlic powder

$^1/_2$ teaspoon sea salt

$^1/_4$ teaspoon black pepper

1 tablespoon pesto dressing or 1 handful basil leaves, optional

directions
Cut cauliflower into 3 inch pieces and steam until soft. Add to blender, reserve steam water. Add all other ingredients and blend, slowly, pouring additional steam water as necessary.

Less water makes a mash potato-like consistency. More water (or vegetable broth) can reduce this recipe to a soup. A hint of basil from the optional ingredients makes this dish really pop with unexpected flavor!

Thai Style Coconut Curry ○

This dish is a delightful way to use up all the veggies you have at the moment. This is one of the only recipes that I suggest using a store-bought Thai curry paste for its unique flavor. They are usually pretty cheap in Asian markets, however, you can find a more expensive version by Thai Kitchen in Whole Food (Stamps), Sprouts, and Berkeley Bowl.

5 cups fresh chopped vegetables (carrots, bell pepper, potato, broccoli, snap peas, onion, zucchini)

1 can coconut milk

1 tablespoon coconut oil

1 tablespoon curry paste

1 tablespoon coconut sugar or sweetener of your choice

1 tablespoon tamari or coconut aminos

2 tablespoons fresh basil leaves, chopped/shredded/ julienne cut

directions
Heat coconut oil on medium in a large pot. Add curry paste and stir two minutes or until fragrant. Add coconut milk; bring to simmer on medium-high heat. Stir in sugar and tamari. Add vegetables; simmer 5 to 7 minutes or until vegetables are tender-crisp. Remove from heat. Stir in basil. Serve with rice.

Simple Sweet Potato
(for the Babies... And You!)

8 sweet potatoes

directions
Preheat oven to 400°F. Pierce clean potatoes sever times with a fork. Place on baking sheet and roast for 40-60 minutes.

When done, a fork can be inserted through them easily. Remove from oven and allow to cool. Serve immediately or reserve in the refrigerator for an easy pre-cooked veggie to eat at home or on the go.

The skin should be easy to remove if you or your little ones prefer it that way.

Cooked Greens

These greens are made from any kind of leafy green like kale, collard, chard, dandelion, beet greens (from the beets you juice), or bok choy. I highly suggest that you avoid cooking spinach, as it changes its beneficial properties.

1 bunch cheapest organic greens

2 garlic cloves

1 tablespoon sunflower oil

salt

directions

Remove as much stem as possible if cooking thicker leaves. Stack leaves on top of each other, then roll together. Slice strings of leaves to create delicate and easy to chew strips.

Heat oil in cast iron skillet or undamaged non-stick pan. Using garlic press, chop or mince garlic and drop into oil. Add a sprinkle of salt to enhance cooking and flavor. When garlic becomes aromatic, add sliced greens and stir to coat evenly. Continue stirring 5-10 minutes depending on the texture of the vegetables. They should be soft, but not overcooked.

For collard greens, I suggest chopping them into small pieces and blanching in hot boiling water for 5 minutes. Drain, then sauté as described. This softens the collard greens so that you do not need to sauté them as long to get the texture you desire.

Roasted Eggplant Soup

When eggplant is in season it is easy to find at the farmers market in large amounts for very little per pound.

1 large Italian eggplant (The big oval dark purple kind, not the emoji one!)

1 onion

1 tomato, diced

1 liter vegetable stock

1 can tomato paste

2 handfuls fresh cilantro leaves

3 garlic cloves

juice of 1/2 lemon

2 tablespoons sunflower oil

1 teaspoon salt, more to taste

1 teaspoon ground black pepper

1 teaspoon smoked paprika

1 small fresh sage leaf, optional

directions

Preheat oven to 400°F. Pierce the eggplant and place on a baking sheet. Roast until soft all the way through (about 30-45 minutes based on the size of the eggplant). It will look limp and wilted when done. Remove from oven and allow to cool. Once the eggplant is cool, carefully remove the skin and scrape the insides into a bowl. Take about 1/4 of the cooked eggplant and chop into small, bite-size pieces. Set aside.

Dice the onions and add them to a large sauce pan with the heated oil. Sprinkle the onions with the salt as they cook over medium heat. Add the tomato, garlic, tomato paste, pepper, and paprika. Cook about 5 minutes. Add remaining eggplant and toss with the spice paste. Add the veggie stock and optional sage leaf. Cover and simmer 10 minutes. Puree with an immersion blender to get a thin soup base. Add more water, as needed, to reach your desired consistency. Add reserved eggplant chunks and lemon. Sprinkle with chopped fresh cilantro when serving.

Coconut Yams

I absolutely love the recipe that Bryant Terry shared in
Vegan Soul Kitchen. It has become a family favorite and
a welcomed delight when I was head chef at the youth
culinary arts program at the YMCA San Francisco. Here is
my version.

6-8 garnet yams (or
whichever sweet potato
variety is cheapest)

4 tablespoons coconut sugar
or maple syrup

1/2 can of coconut milk (other
1/2 reserved for blending, as
needed)

1/2 teaspoon sea salt

2 tablespoons coconut oil

directions
Preheat oven to 400°F. Cut
the yams into 1 inch chunks.
Place on a parchment-lined
baking sheet and roast in the
oven for 40 minutes. Check
every 10 minutes to prevent
burning.

Remove roasted yams from
oven and place in food
processor with the remaining
ingredients. Use additional
coconut milk to achieve your
desired consistency.

Ayurvedic Green Beans

This recipe also works nicely with asparagus!

2 cups green beans, ends
removed, cut into 2 inch pieces

or 2 cups asparagus spears,
tough ends removed

1 tablespoon coconut oil

1/4 teaspoon cumin seeds

1/4 teaspoon black mustard
seeds

pinch cayenne, optional

pinch sea salt

directions
Heat coconut oil in a skillet.
Add the seeds and cayenne.
Heat until they begin to
pop. Add the green beans
and salt. Stir and allow to
cook for 5 minutes. Turn off
heat, cover, and let sit for 2
minutes before serving.

Ital Stew O

The name of this recipe loosely describes almost any combo of veggies simmered in coconut curry, island style. Traditionally, it contains beans or tofu, however, for our purposes, these are optional, as they are heavier and more complicated to digest.

2 golden potatoes, chopped into small cubes

1 onion, sliced

1 carrot, cut into thin rounds

1 cup sliced mushrooms

2 cups, chopped seasonal veggies (green beans, broccoli, etc.)

cooked lentils or other legumes, optional

$1/2$ can coconut milk

1 tablespoon curry

2 teaspoons garam masala, optional

$1/4$ teaspoon sea salt

directions

It is possible to create this dish without cooking oil. Simply add all ingredients except coconut milk to the pot and add enough water to cover them halfway. Turn on heat and monitor the water to make sure the water does not completely evaporate. Add more if necessary, stirring often. Once vegetables are almost completely cooked, add coconut milk, and stir. Cover and let sit while the veggies absorb the coconut milk flavor. Serve over brown rice for a traditional Ital experience.

Stewed Greens (traditional style)

2 cups of **veggie broth or water**

2-3 large bunches of your favorite greens (the cheapest organic ones)

4 cloves garlic, sliced thinly

1 onion, sliced

2 teaspoons liquid smoke

1 teaspoon chopped sun-dried tomatoes

salt and pepper, to taste

directions
If cooking greens with a hearty stem, remove the leaves and discard the thick stems. Cut or tear the leaves into bite size pieces. I sometimes create long ribbons of greens by making a chiffonade. Either way, the recipe works. Bring the broth or water to a boil with the sliced onion and garlic. Add the remaining ingredients, cover, and turn to low. Simmer for about 20 minutes or until the greens are soft enough for you to enjoy. Drink the broth after enjoying the greens!

Jerk Jackfruit

1 cup water

$^1/_2$ cup tamari or soy aminos

3 tablespoons coconut sugar or 2 tablespoons maple syrup

2 tablespoons rum, optional

2 onions, chopped

2 anise seeds, optional

4 teaspoons Jerk Seasoning (*Chapter Thirteen - Essential Spices, Blends, and Easy Hacks*)

4 lbs fresh jackfruit, skinned and cubed or 4 cans jackfruit

directions
Combine all ingredients except for jackfruit in a dutch oven and bring to a boil. Add the jackfruit. Return to a boil, then cover, reduce heat, and simmer for 20 minutes. Remove lid and stir, cooking uncovered for another 5 minutes. Serve over Brown Coco Rice (*Chapter Ten - Cooked Grains*).

Lightly Cooked Zucchini Noodles

Here's a super healthy noodle dish that the entire family loves.

2 large zucchinis

1 cup sliced mushrooms

2 shallots, chopped

2 garlic cloves, pressed

1 tablespoon sun-dried tomatoes

salt and pepper, to taste

1 tablespoon olive oil

sprig of basil

directions

Hold the zucchini at the stalk and use a veggie peeler to peel it into flat thick noodles.

Heat the oil in the skillet. Cook the shallots and garlic with a sprinkle of salt until fragrant. Add the mushrooms and sauté for five minutes. Add zucchini noodles and sun-dried tomatoes. Stir until evenly mixed.

Cover, remove from heat, and allow to cook for 5-10 minutes longer. Uncover and season with salt and pepper. Use basil as a garnish (can be chopped finely and sprinkled on top).

Zucchini Pad Thai

This recipe is fragrant and full of flavor. I also recommend trying it with spaghetti squash (when in season), another cheap source of plant-based greatness.. If you find yourself short on time and ingredients, simply cook the zucchini noodles lightly, and toss with un-peanut sauce (*Chapter Eight - Roughage*). Another way to modify this recipe is to add cooked bean thread noodles, which are very cheap. Cut up your spiralized zucchini noodles and bean threads to make them easier to consume after cooking.

2 green or yellow zucchini squashes, spiralized or peeled into noodles

1 small onion or several shallots, chopped

6 garlic cloves, pressed

2 tablespoons sesame oil

2 tablespoons tamari, soy aminos, or coconut aminos

directions

Sauté your onions, shallots, and garlic in sesame oil until soft and fragrant. Add zucchini noodles and tamari/soy/coconut aminos and stir. Cook for 5 minutes on high heat, then remove from heat.

The noodles will continue to soften as they cool, so serve immediately to avoid soggy noodles.

Struggle Potatoes
by Lateefah Simon

4 Russet potatoes

1 bell pepper, chopped

1 white onion, diced

$1/2$ teaspoon curry powder
(sub $1/4$ teaspoon garlic
powder if less spice is
desired)

salt and pepper, to taste

olive oil

directions

Cut up your onions and bell
peppers. Put them into the
skillet. Your skillet needs to
be hot with olive oil. Three
teaspoons should work. Stir
until your house smells good
(about 20 seconds). Add cut
potatoes.

The smaller you cut the
potatoes, the quicker they
will be done. The trick is to
turn the heat on medium
and let them cook. Listen to
one Mary J song and turn
them over or stir. Then, let
them cook again for another
4 to 5 minutes.

Add some salt and pepper.
Your babies might not like
curry, so only put a little in.
Replace with garlic powder if
you are not ready for curry.

Once the potatoes have a
little bit of brown on each
side, put a half a cup (baby
ikea cup) of water and put
the lid on for about a minute.

*Add more potatoes and
onions, etc. if you want this
to last a couple of days. I
add greens, tomatoes, and
mushrooms to this treat each
day, to give it some newness.
But for less than five dollars,
you will be eating hella good.*

Tostones

1-2 green plantains (feeds a momma and toddler)

preferred frying oil, enough to nearly cover the plantain slices while frying

sea salt

ketchup or dressings (*Chapter Eight - Roughage*) **for dipping**

directions
Heat oil in a cast iron or non-stick skillet. Remove the peel of the plantain like a pro by cutting off both ends.

Slice a shallow seam down the length of the plantain that pierces the skin and just slightly penetrates the inner plantain fruit. Reach into the seam to rip the peel away from the fruit. Slice circles or ovals as thin as you can for quick frying. Add the slices one by one to the hot oil, and turn down to medium. Turn plantains as they become golden yellow on both sides. Remove promptly and drain on a paper towel. Sprinkle with sea salt.

Fried Maduros / Sweet Plantains

As a small side, this recipe is enough for two people or as many as four.

2 ripe plantains

2 tablespoons coconut oil

directions
Peel maduros and slice into ¹/₂ inch rounds. Heat oil in a cast iron skillet. Oil is ready when adding a plantain causes it to sizzle. Add as many plantains as will fit so your skillet is covered with plantain but no pieces are on top of each other. Turn down heat to medium-low. Check often and turn plantains with a fork as they darken. Remove and drain on paper towels when evenly brown. Allow to cool slightly and serve.

PRO TIP

If reusing your fried plantain oil for multiple plantain creations, fry the tostones before frying maduros. The oil tastes slightly sweeter after maduros and can change the flavor of the tostones.

Tandoori Cauliflower

You can still make this recipe even if you don't have the specific tandoori spice powder. Get creative and mix any combo of the tandoori contents (ginger, cumin, coriander, paprika, turmeric, and cayenne).

1 head of cauliflower

1 tablespoon tandoori spice

1 tablespoon sunflower oil

$^1/_2$ teaspoon salt

directions
Preheat oven to 400°F. Cut cauliflower into drumsticks and bite-size pieces. In a large bowl, add cauliflower, spices, and oil. Cover with an equal size bowl or plate and shake until evenly coated. Place cauliflower onto a parchment-lined baking sheet and bake on the center rack for 20 minutes. Turn cauliflower pieces. Bake for another 5-10 minutes.

Oven-roasted Maduros / Sweet Plantains

any number of ripe sweet plantains

melted coconut oil for brushing

ground cinnamon

directions
Preheat oven to 350°F. Remove peel. Cut each plantain in halves or thirds, about 3 inches each segment. Place one piece at a time on flat end and slice into quarters, making strips. Arrange strips on parchment-lined baking sheet. Bake for 10 minutes, turning the strips on their second side halfway through. Check and if necessary, turn strips and bake for an additional 5-10 minutes. Remove from oven and brush with coconut oil. Sprinkle with a few pinches of cinnamon.

Chapter Ten

Cooked Grains: Heavier than Veggies

Grains are heavier than cooked veggies, so eat them after a salad or digestion prep. Remember carrots, jicama, celery, cucumber, and red bell pepper sticks are fine ways to prep for meals! Grains combine well with cooked veggies, though mixing with nuts, seeds, and legumes (beans) make a more complex and heavy combination.

Grains are heavier than cooked veggies, so eat these after a salad or digestion prep.

A word on grains: I left out all the wheat family grains. And to be honest, I'm not too excited about most cooked grains mainly because it is filler food for poor diets. I also throw some corn recipes in here because organic corn without GMOs and pesticides was a nutritious staple for many prior to colonization. If you're curious, check out the Iroquois legend, *Three Sisters*, based on corn, beans, and squash.

Vegan Tamales

Ok, so actually I'm not going to teach you HOW to make a tamal in this cookbook. You gotta go get that info from abuela. I was taught by the legendary Marlene Sanchez, my teenage co-worker at the Center for Young Women's Development in San Francisco. The point of this recipe is to outline some excellent ingredients to put inside these tamales made of lard-free masa!

Cashew cheese, zucchini, bell pepper

Cashew cheese, portobello mushroom, heart of palm

Cashew cheese, chipotle peppers in adobo, heart of palm

directions
Make cashew cheese according to the recipe (*Chapter Eight - Roughage*) and seek a thicker consistency. Slice the veggies nice and thin so you can add a few of each to the tamal. Seal in hojas and steam as usual.

Whole Oats While You Sleep

We discovered this method on the back of a WIC oatmeal container! It's so awesome if you want to have a meal ready to go to take for lunch. Generally, I don't advise eating oatmeal for breakfast unless you start with a breakfast salad. Grains and nuts are on the heavier end of the food chart.

$^1/_2$ cup rolled oats

$^2/_3$ cup non-dairy milk (see cashew milk or oat milk)

$^1/_3$ cup coconut milk yogurt, optional

1 tablespoon chia seeds or flax seed meal

$^1/_2$ teaspoon vanilla extract

1 tablespoon maple syrup or honey

mixed raw nuts and seeds, optional

directions
Place all ingredients in jar. Shake well. Leave in refrigerator overnight.

Alternatives

Add $^1/_4$ frozen, fresh, or dried berries. This isn't the greatest combo digestively, but if you are feeling healthy it is fine to splurge a bit.

Add $^1/_4$ cup raisins, $^1/_3$ cup shredded carrot, and $^1/_4$ teaspoon ground cinnamon for a hearty change to the usual oatmeal routine.

Add $^1/_2$ banana, sliced.

Add $^1/_4$ cup unsweetened shredded coconut.

The possibilities are endless!

Coco Rice

This is a perfect use of WIC brown rice. I learned it from Bryant Terry's *Vegan Soul Kitchen*. I have met a few home chefs, Lateefah Simon included, who use a variation of this recipe in their daily food routines.

2 cups or 1-16 ounces package of WIC-approved brown rice

1 can coconut milk

2 1/2 cups water

1/2 teaspoon salt

1 tablespoon unrefined coconut oil

1/3 cup unsweetened shredded coconut

directions

Add all ingredients except oil to rice cooker and press cook. When finished, gently stir in coconut oil so that it is not cooked in the process.

Of course, this is totally possible to do without a rice cooker. Simply add water, coconut milk, and salt to a pot. Bring to a boil.

Add rice and shredded coconut, cover, and reduce to low. Cook for at least an hour before checking. Remove from heat and allow to continue cooking for 10 more minutes. Stir in coconut oil and fluff with a fork.

Quinoa Batter

The following recipes use a super simple quinoa batter that is high in protein and unlikely to cause allergies unlike wheat-based foods.

Pancakes

1 cup quinoa, soaked overnight, drained, and rinsed

1 cup water

2 teaspoons baking soda

1/4 teaspoon sea salt

1-2 tablespoons coconut sugar or maple syrup, to sweeten

coconut oil for coating skillet

directions
Heat a skillet on medium.

Blend all ingredients until a pancake batter consistency is reached. Add more water if necessary. Pour directly from blender pitcher onto hot oiled skillet in your desired amount for pancakes. Flip pancakes when the bubbles appear across the entire surface.

These can be made into savory pancakes by skipping the sugar and adding leftover cooked veggies that you blend with the batter or dice very thinly.

Pizza

1 cup quinoa, soaked overnight, drained, and rinsed

1/4 cup water

1 tablespoon sunflower oil

1 teaspoon baking powder

1/4 teaspoon salt

SAUCE AND TOPPINGS

pesto (*Chapter Eight - Roughage*)

jar of marinara sauce

sliced veggies

cashew parmesan

Daiya cheese (somewhat cost prohibitive)

directions
Preheat the oven to 425°F. Place the soaked quinoa into blender with water, salt, and baking powder. Process for 1-2 minutes until smooth. Cut parchment paper to line an 8 or 9 inch cake pan. Spray or brush oil on the parchment paper lining and pour batter into the cake pan. Bake for 15 minutes. Remove from oven and carefully flip the crust. Bake for another 15 minutes.

Top the pizza, as desired. Once you have added toppings to pizza crust, bake for an additional 5-10 minutes.

Quinoa Porridge

This is a nice easy versatile meal that can give your porridge routine some variety. Make a large batch of quinoa in advance and store in the fridge. Reheat your desired amount of servings for a hot meal or serve cold.

$1/2$ cup cooked quinoa (hot or cold)

$1/4$ cup non-dairy milk

2 teaspoons maple syrup

$1/4$ teaspoon ground

cinnamon

directions
Combine all ingredients, stir, serve!

Quinoa Sushi Bowl
(single serving)

$3/4$ cup cooked quinoa

$1/4$ avocado

1 teaspoon tamari or coconut aminos

1 teaspoon grated fresh ginger

1 nori sheet cut into small strips

$1/2$ teaspoon toasted sesame oil

directions
Mix all ingredients in with your cooked quinoa and enjoy the delightful flavor of sushi with added health benefits and zero white rice.

Heirloom Grits aka Blue Cornmeal
by Mari Posa

Corn is an indigenous staple of North and South America. This recipe was learned from Edward Box III of Ignacio, CO. This traditional hot blue corn grits recipe appears in many dishes such as atol (Mexico) and atol de elote (El Salvador, Guatemala, and Honduras). It is also known as blue corn mush (Navajo Nation), and blue cornmeal (Southern Ute Nation in the Four Corners). If blue cornmeal is not available, substitute yellow corn grits and enjoy the more common version of grits.

1/4 cup blue cornmeal

2 tablespoons coconut oil

water

salt, to taste

directions
Heat coconut oil in a skillet until oil gets wavy. Slowly add cornmeal and stir rapidly until you smell it cooking like popcorn. Slowly add water while stirring, to reach desired consistency. Add salt to taste.

Sticky Rice Buns

I discovered this recipe by accident when I soaked glutinous rice instead of regular long grain. I blended the rice and discovered it smelled and tasted like the dim sum recipes I grew up eating in San Francisco, but which I can no longer eat because they include ingredients I cut out of my healthy lifestyle. Makes approximately 1 dozen buns, depending on the size of the mold.

1 cup sweet rice, soaked overnight, drained

$1/4$ - $3/4$ cup water for consistency

1 teaspoon baking powder

$1/4$ teaspoon salt

oil for cupcake pan or mold

FILLING

seasoned carrot juicer pulp

Chinese five-spice powder

coconut oil

directions
Take at least a cup of carrot juice pulp from your juicer. Lightly sauté for a couple minutes in coconut oil with $1/2$ teaspoon to 1 teaspoon of spices. Add salt, to taste.

You can also make your filling from finely chopped cooked veggies. Think of the leftovers that need to be repurposed! Any of the veggie patty fillings from this chapter, or bean dishes from *Chapter Eleven - Protein Finale*, are possible fillings as well.

Preheat oven to 400°F. Blend soaked rice and add water, slowly, until a smooth batter is created. Line cupcake pan or grease silicone cupcake molds. Fill each mold a $1/4$ of the way with batter. Add filling. Pour enough batter to cover filling, up to $3/4$ full in the mold. Bake for 25 minutes. Allow to cool before serving.

Doubles

This is possibly the most complicated recipe in the book. But, there's no way I'm not gonna share this mouthwatering fry bread delicacy with the world, especially since I learned how to make a gluten-free version. Here's the thing: I use a bread machine to make the dough. <drops mic>

Dough (Bara)
(adapted to be gluten-free from Caribbean Vegan by Taymer Mason)

1 1/4 teaspoons active dry yeast

1 1/2 teaspoons brown sugar

1 1/2 cups warm water

3 cups gluten-free all-purpose flour

1/2 cup chickpea flour

1 1/2 teaspoons baking powder

3/4 teaspoon salt

1 teaspoon Madras curry powder

1 teaspoon ground cumin

sunflower oil

directions
Add ingredients to bread machine. Press buttons to set dough. Walk away and do something else (about 2 hours). Return to dough that has risen.

While bread machine is making magic, cook the filling.

Filling

1/4 - 1/2 cup sunflower oil

2-3 tablespoons curry powder

1 large onion, diced

2 teaspoons minced garlic

1 teaspoon ground allspice

1 teaspoon ground nutmeg spice

1 1/2 teaspoon smoked paprika

2 teaspoons fresh or dried thyme

1 teaspoon cumin spice

1 teaspoon white pepper

2 cans chickpeas, drained (or 1 cup WIC dry chickpeas, soaked overnight and cooked 1-2 hrs)

2 cups veggie stock or water

1/2 -1 teaspoon cayenne pepper, optional

2 green onions, chopped

2 tablespoons chopped parsley

salt to taste

directions

Heat up large sauce pan with oil. Add onions, garlic, thyme, cumin spice, allspice, smoked paprika, nutmeg and curry powder. Stir occasionally for about 2-3 minutes until onion is translucent.

Add potatoes, stir, and sauté for about 2-3 minutes. Add water if necessary to prevent burning.

Add chickpeas, green onion and stock. Bring to a boil and let it simmer until sauce thickens. This may take about 18 minutes. Add parsley, salt, and pepper until desired flavor is reached. The texture should resemble stew. Serve warm.

Make small balls of dough. Flatten with oiled hands. Fry in 1 1/2 inches oil on medium high heat. Use the pattern of 5-10-5: 5 minutes on first side, 10 minutes on second side, and 5 more minutes on first side. Cool on paper towels.

Jamaican Veggie Patty

This is another complicated recipe I love. It is a great way to make use of WIC lentils, and a fun food for kids that packs a lot of veggies. This is a very versatile baked delight for which I longed to find a gluten-free version while living in and visiting Brooklyn. This recipe uses gluten-free all-purpose flour and pastry flour instead of wheat flour. Doing so changes the cost a bit, but since I figured out how to make my own gluten-free flour blend, I was able to keep the cost of my baked goods low.

Lentil Filling
Use leftover Mesir Wot (*Chapter Eleven - Protein Finale*) or create the following:

1/2 cup dry green (or brown) lentils

2 tablespoons coconut oil

1/2 onion, diced

2 clove garlic, minced

2 tablespoons green bell pepper, diced

1/4 teaspoon red pepper flakes or fresh hot pepper, optional

1 teaspoon ground cumin

1 tablespoon curry powder (Madras preferred)

1 teaspoon white pepper

2 cups water

1 tablespoon tomato paste

1 tablespoon soy aminos or tamari sauce

1 teaspoon Worcestershire sauce (vegan, if possible)

salt, to taste

2 tablespoons crushed rice krispies

directions

Quick soak the lentils in 1 cup of boiling water for 30 minutes. Drain. In skillet, heat oil and sauté onion, garlic, bell pepper, hot pepper, lentils, cumin, curry, and white pepper over medium heat for about 3-5 minutes until onions are soft.

Stir in 1 cup water, tomato paste, soy/tamari, and Worcestershire sauce. Cover, reduce heat, and cook for 20 minutes. Stir in additional water (about 1/2 cup, as necessary).

Turn heat to low and cook another 10 minutes until thickened. Add salt to taste and rice krispies mix. Stir until paste consistency forms. Remove from heat and cool.

Veggie Filling

(adapted from *Vegan Soul Kitchen* by Bryant Terry)

1 tablespoon coconut oil

$1/2$ cup diced onion

$1/8$ teaspoon ground cinnamon

$1/4$ teaspoon ground allspice

$1/2$ teaspoon ground cumin

$1/4$ teaspoon minced habanero or scotch bonnet pepper,optional

sea salt

2 cloves garlic, minced

$3/4$ cup canned coconut milk

$1/4$ cup diced carrots or carrot juice pulp

$1/4$ cup diced potatoes

$1/2$ cup green peas

$1/2$ cup corn

$1/2$ cup shredded cabbage

1 tablespoon minced fresh thyme

1 tablespoon lemon juice

$1/2$ teaspoon ground white pepper

directions

Sautée the onion and $1/2$ teaspoon salt with the spices and optional pepper in the coconut oil over medium heat. Stir occasionally for about 5-7 minutes or until onions are caramelized.

Add garlic and cook another few minutes. Add coconut milk and carrots and potatoes, cover, reduce heat and simmer until tender. Stir in remaining ingredients and cook for 5 minutes. Season with salt and pepper, as needed. Remove from heat and allow seasoning to settle.

Short Crust Pastry with Turmeric

(adapted from *Vegan Soul Kitchen* by Terry Bryant to be gluten-free)

1 ³/₄ cups all-purpose gluten-free flour (if gluten is not an issue, please use whichever wheat flour you prefer)

1 cup gluten-free pastry flour (It is possible to use all-purpose flour if you can't find/make pastry flour.)

2 teaspoons turmeric

¹/₂ teaspoon fine sea salt

³/₄ cup chilled coconut oil

2 teaspoons apple cider vinegar

¹/₂ cup plus 2 tablespoons ice water

directions

Make sure the coconut oil was refrigerated 20 minutes prior. Spoon the cold oil in small scoops into a bowl containing 1 ¹/₂ cups all-purpose gluten-free flour, the pastry flour, and turmeric well combined, reserving the remaining ¹/₄ cup all-purpose flour. Use a pastry knife to cut the cold oil into the dough until the texture is like sand.

Mix the vinegar and water, and add gently to the dough, tablespoon by tablespoon. Stir just enough for the dough to form away from the sides of the bowl, but do not overwork (and do not let your stir-happy three-year-old mix). Mold the dough into a ball. Press flat. Wrap in plastic and chill for an hour.

Preheat the oven to 350°F. Dust a surface with your reserved flour. Roll out the chilled dough to about ¹/₈ inch thickness. Use a cup or bowl to cut circles into the dough. Place filling on one half of circle; then fold the other side over to create a closed pocket. Seal by crimping the edges with a fork. Transfer the patties to a lined baking sheet and bake for 30 minutes or until golden brown. Allow to cool slightly before serving.

Mac n Cheese

1 large delicata squash, seeded or about $1/2$ peeled butternut squash, seeded

1 cup raw or sprouted sunflower seeds

2 cloves garlic, pressed

1 teaspoon sea salt

1 teaspoon turmeric for color

$1/4$ cup sunflower oil (or high quality oil of your choice)

$1/4$ teaspoon white pepper

2 tablespoons nutritional yeast

directions

Remove the skin from the butternut squash, but leave the skin on the delicata. Remove all the seeds from the squash you are using. Cut the squash into 2 inch pieces. Steam until soft (about 20 minutes).

Optional step: Soak the sunflower seeds in water while the squash is steaming.

Drain. I usually just blend them without soaking and the texture is great, however, I use a very powerful blender. Soaking may help if you are using a conventional household blender or food processor.

Place all ingredients except oil into the blender. Pulse until the consistency starts to get doughy. Slowly add oil while continuing to blend using the opening at the top of the blender. If necessary, stop blender and scrape down the sides to insure complete blending. The sauce should be creamy.

For this recipe: I use one package of gluten-free elbow macaroni. After noodles are cooked and drained, I use a spatula to get all the cheese sauce out of the blender and combine with the noodles until evenly coated.

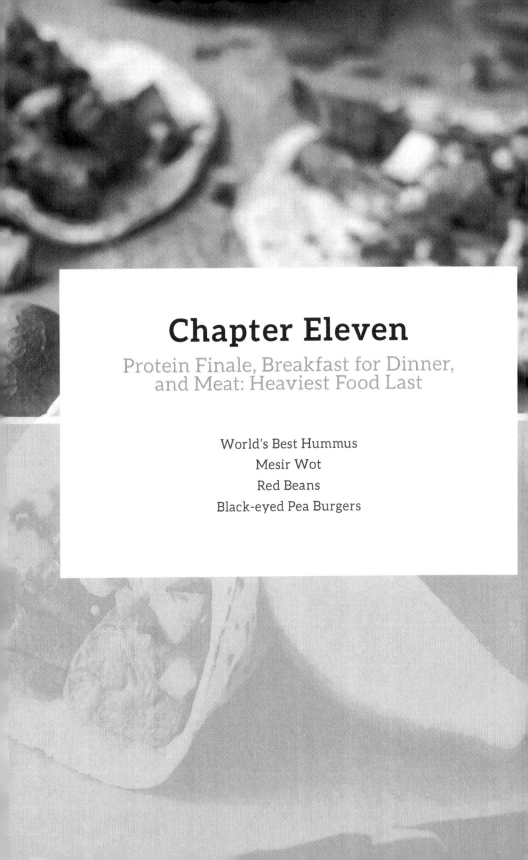

Chapter Eleven

Protein Finale, Breakfast for Dinner,
and Meat: Heaviest Food Last

World's Best Hummus

Mesir Wot

Red Beans

Black-eyed Pea Burgers

Here are some more protein sources if your needs require it. Basically, the nuts and seeds are my recommended source for protein because they are less acidic than legumes. That said, these bean-based options are perfect for anyone in need of denser concentrated protein. When I was pregnant, Issa had me eating Mesir Wot every damn day. Thank goodness my college squadmate hooked me up with that good Eritrean cooking lesson.

> These bean-based options are perfect for anyone in need of denser concentrated protein.

PRO TIP

I always use a couple inches of kombu seaweed when cooking my beans. This makes the texture super appealing while adding some good sea vegetable minerals.

World's Best Hummus

2-15 ounces cans chickpeas or 1 1/2 cups dried beans, soaked and cooked in advance

1 yellow onion, chopped

3 garlic cloves, pressed

1 tablespoon sunflower oil

juice of 1 lemon

salt and pepper, to taste

directions

Sauté the onion in the oil and sprinkle with salt while cooking. Once translucent, add garlic and cook until slightly charred.

Add sautéed mixture, chickpeas, lemon juice, pinches of salt and pepper to food processor. Blend until combined but still somewhat chunky. Taste and season, if necessary.

Mesir Wot

Soooo... Let's talk about Mesir Wot dish. First, let me start by saying I do NOT love legumes. Story for another time. HOWEVER, while pregnant with my magical earthling, Issa, I HAD to eat this dish every day or else. I love it because it is easier to digest than other legumes (like split peas), especially when you soak overnight. It also cooks very fast!

Base Sauce

2 cups chopped onion

3 tablespoons oil

2 tablespoons berbere plus 1 tablespoon water

8 ounces chopped or pureed tomatoes

2 teaspoons minced garlic

2 teaspoons ground cardamom

directions
Sauté onions in oil until translucent. Add garlic and tomatoes and cook for 5 minutes. Make a paste by mixing berbere with water. Add berbere paste to pan and stir for 5 minutes. Add cardamom and additional water, if necessary. Simmer for 2 more minutes until the sauce thickens.

Red Lentils

1 cup lentils, washed, soaked overnight, and drained

directions
Add lentils to base sauce. Add an additional cup of water and stir. Bring to a boil. Carefully check the texture of the lentils. Cook uncovered until soft. Add salt to taste before serving.

Red Beans ⟳
(remixed by Baba Vincent)

My father and I discovered this recipe while trying to figure out how best to use WIC beans. I had so many beans after the baby was born and I wasn't particularly fond of legumes. Still not a fan. But this recipe is delicious and I want you bean lovers to enjoy it.

1 cup dry pinto beans, washed, and soaked overnight

1 1/2 cups chopped onion

1/2 cup coconut oil

1 cup canned whole tomatoes, drained and chopped

1 tablespoon tomato paste

1 large clove garlic, minced

1/4 teaspoon cayenne pepper

1/4 teaspoon white pepper

1/2 teaspoon salt

directions
Combine the soaked beans with 8 cups of water and bring to a boil. Reduce heat to low and add 1/4 cup onion and simmer (partly covered) for about an hour until the beans soften. Drain and set aside. In a large skillet, heat the oil and sauté the rest of the onion until soft. Add the remaining ingredients, mix well, and simmer until the liquid evaporates.

Add the beans to the skillet and cook uncovered for 5-10 minutes, stirring frequently.

Black-eyed Pea Burgers

Have you ever wondered what to do with all this WIC black-eyed peas (or any excess legumes)? Make black-eyed pea burgers! This is another opportunity to incorporate juicer pulp from your veggies like carrots, beets, kale, celery, or fennel.

2 cups black-eyed peas, cooked (or use canned)

1 head Napa cabbage

1 green bell pepper, diced

2 shallots or 1 onion, diced

2 garlic cloves, pressed

1/2 cup chopped carrots or carrot juicer pulp

3 flax eggs

1 tablespoon nutritional yeast, optional

1/2 teaspoon sea salt

1/4 teaspoon ground black pepper

1/4 teaspoon smoked paprika

2 tablespoons sunflower oil

additional oil for frying

directions

Heat one tablespoon of the oil in a skillet. Sauté the shallots and garlic with a pinch of sea salt. Add bell pepper and carrots. Cook for about 5 minutes, stirring often.

Add sautéed veggies to food processor with remaining ingredients and process until smooth, but somewhat grainy.

Let batter rest in refrigerator for at least 30 minutes to an hour. This will make it easier to handle when ready to cook.

Heat additional oil for frying in a non-stick pan. Roll the batter into balls and press lightly into burger shape. Press with spatula if necessary. Turn with fork or spatula after three minutes. Allow to cook for another three minutes on the second side. Drain on a paper towel before serving in a Napa cabbage leaf.

Now that you know all about timing and having the heaviest foods last, you are probably wondering why most well-known "break" "fast" foods are so heavy. This is the man tryna keep your energy down. Trust me. So go on ahead and consume heavier foods as your last meal of the day, following a big salad, of course!

FAVORITE BREAKFAST FOR DINNER RECIPES

Quinoa Pancakes (*Chapter Ten -Cooked Grains*)

Vegan Tamales (*Chapter Ten - Cooked Grains*)

Doubles (*Chapter Ten - Cooked Grains*)

Avocado Dip (*Chapter Eight - Roughage*) on Toast

Finally, let's talk about meat. You were probably like, "Wait! Where's the meat in this cookbook?" Here's why I saved it for last. It is the densest food you can eat, so have it last, after your big salad. Meat takes the longest to digest completely, so you have the long fasting/sleeping period to break it down. It is also the hardest to combine with anything else, thus simpler combinations are better (e.g. meat and vegetables. Lots of vegetables). Mixing it with grains, say a sandwich or rice, would make it most complex. It will zap your energy, so eat it last and then get some rest!

It is the densest food you can eat, so have it last, after your big salad.

It's a personal decision whether to eat animal protein or not.

For the purposes of this book I left out recipes using meat because it is the most expensive thing you can buy. I want to leave you with a survival guide for getting through the month gracefully and cost-effectively on $200 per person and $357 per baby mama and baby. That's not much to work with. I guarantee that the eating style and recipes provided will keep you alive and vibrantly healthy for that amount. I'm counting meat as extra because it is not absolutely necessary for your survival. Wait, what?

Here's what I'm saying. People ask, "No meat?" What about protein? Refer to the options in *Chapter Eleven – Protein Finale, Breakfast for Dinner, and Meat: Heaviest Food Last,* and consider all the nut and seed pâtés that are protein-packed and inflammation-reducing. Meat can't do that. And just how much protein is necessary for your daily nutrition needs? It may be less than you think. Plus, consider that protein is actually the building blocks of every single food, so everything you eat is giving you protein.

Consider all the nut and seed pâtés that are protein-packed and inflammation reducing. Meat can't do that.

Here's my final beef with beef. We used to eat animals as ancient humans for some awesome benefits – amino acids which are the omega 3-6-9s, the essential fatty acids. Well, the reason these healthy aminos were present in meat was because the animals eating them were grazing on luscious grasses. You know the saying: "Vegetarians taste better." We were humans getting the health benefits of vegetarianism from the original vegetarians we ate. Nowadays, you gotta examine your meat's upbringing. If the animal was factory farmed, most likely, it didn't eat any fresh veggies ever. It might not have even ever walked and developed a healthy metabolism. Also, it may have been inhumanely handled, and lived in unsanitary conditions. For this reason, it has been pumped with antibiotics and possibly sprayed down with ammonia after it died in its own feces. The meat probably lacks the protein benefits it is supposed to deliver, and besides, it's basically chemically treated garbage. I haven't even gotten into the genetically-engineered super meat species saga. I'm not

Nowadays, you gotta examine your meat's upbringing... It might not have even ever walked and developed a healthy metabolism.

here to go into meat dangers. I'm here to help you make better decisions that reduce harm and increase your power. If you want to have meat, get that free-range, grass-fed, NORMAL animal product. Only. Since that's about to cost more than the Foster Farms option, make it affordable by splurging once or twice a week. You will be perfectly fine (and healthier) when you consume less meat.

Chapter Twelve

Sweet Treats: Breads, Cookies, Cakes, and Raw Delicacies

Enjoy sweets as often as you like as soon as you reduce your harm by kicking out the bad sugars. Here are some baked and raw recipes for indulgence. Usually, raw desserts can be eaten with fruits or after a raw salad meal. Whatever you do, just remember to eat fruit with fruit. You may find that having a raw, fruit-based dessert after eating heavier foods can create gas bubbles.

Chickpea Flour

Dried chickpeas in any amount (Thank you, WIC!)

directions
Process chickpeas in a blender, spice/coffee grinder, or food processor for 2 minutes or so. Dump flour into a large bowl and sift out (with a sieve) the larger hard pieces of peas from the powdery flour. Return the larger pieces to the blender and continue processing until all flour is uniform.

Oat Flour

This is a wonderful gluten-free flour. Some will say oats are not gluten-free, but that is because of cross-contamination, not because oats are a gluten grain. If gluten sensitivity is intense, be sure to find gluten-free oats, free of cross contamination. And use WIC to get all the whole oats you can.

1 cup whole oats = 1 cup oat flour

directions
Place oats in blender or food processor and pulse for a minute until powder like. Stir occasionally between pulsing to make sure all oats are being ground uniformly.

DIY Flour Blend

This is a gluten-free blend to use in place of wheat flours. Back in the day (8 years ago) when I started collecting recipes, it was hella hard to find gluten-free flour mixes or it was craze balls expensive. It's 2017 as I write this final edit on desserts and I just grabbed a pack of GF flour at Trader Joe's... for significantly less than Bob's Red Mill, which was like the only GF flour option back then. This recipe is still a great option for saving $ in the long run because you can find some of the individual flours for cheap at Indian or Asian markets, or even in the bulk section of your local grocery coop. Or even in the bulk section of Whole Food (Stamps), as long as you find a similar item for less and conscientiously mis-label your purchase as something more fiscally sound. IJS. Also, I learned from Gluten-Free Girl that substituting GF flour in a recipe that calls for wheat flour is more consistent when you weigh the flour and use the conversion of 140 grams GF to 1 cup all-purpose flour. You can follow the weight guideline below for creating the flour, or simply convert to cups using the same ratio.

400 grams of whole grain flour (my current mix is $^1/_2$ sorghum and $^1/_2$ millet)

300 grams sweet white rice flour

300 grams potato starch (or any other starch like cornstarch or tapioca starch)

directions
Combine all flours in a large sealable container and shake vigorously!

Unlimited flour reserve for the baking!

Other flours to try

Spelt (contains gluten)

Buckwheat (contains gluten)

Chickpea (cheap in Indian grocery and easy DIY)

Almond Oat (see recipe for using WIC oats)

Ratio to use for combining any kind of non-wheat flour is 40 percent whole grains and 60 percent starches or white rice flour. When using chickpea flour, use as part of the 40 percent whole grain proportion. It can take some experimenting to find the best combo for your particular recipe.

Baba's Chocolate Chip Cookies

3 flax eggs

³/₄ cup coconut flour

³/₄ cup almond flour (or 1 ¹/₂ cup total flour of your choice)

1 teaspoon baking soda

¹/₂ teaspoon salt

¹/₂ cup coconut oil

1 cup coconut sugar

1 teaspoon vanilla

1 cup dairy-free chocolate chips

directions
Heat oven to 350°F. Line a baking sheet with parchment or a silpat you manage to acquire (Story for another time.). Prepare the flax eggs. Beat the oil and sugar until well combined. Ideally it should be a bit fluffy, but I only achieve that result when using an electric mixer. Whisk flour, baking soda, and salt. Set aside.

In another bowl, whisk flax eggs, vanilla, and oil. Add flour mixture gradually to the flax eggs and oil mix. Stir until all ingredients are evenly incorporated. Fold the chocolate chips into the dough. Alternatively, you can use 1 cup of unsweetened coconut flakes instead of chocolate chips, which cuts down on sugar. Use a spring loaded ice cream scoop to place evenly sized dough balls on your parchment or silpat. Bake for 10 minutes. For crispier cookies, bake a few minutes longer. Allow cookies to cool 2 minutes on baking sheet, then transfer to a cooling rack.

Raw Mousse

1 cup raisins, soaked 1 hour in 1 cup water

1 avocado

3 tablespoons maple syrup or more, to taste

1 teaspoon alcohol-free vanilla extract or powder

$^1/_2$ cup carob powder (ok to use cocoa which is not raw)

directions
Remove raisins from the water and keep the water for blending the recipe as it will add to the sweetness. In blender or food processor, combine avocado, raisin water, and maple syrup. Add vanilla and carob gradually.

Can be served as a cute raw dessert on its own or as a spread on top of raw brownies.

Raw Brownies

1 cup pecans or walnuts

1 cup pitted Medjool dates

$^1/_4$ cup raw cacao powder

$^1/_4$ cup cocoa powder

$^1/_3$ cup shredded unsweetened coconut

4 tablespoons maple syrup

1 teaspoon vanilla extract

pinch of salt

directions
Pulse the pecans in the food processor until they become crumbly. Add the dates and continue processing until the mixture clumps. Add the remaining ingredients and process until smooth, but not too creamy that it becomes too sticky to easily remove from the food processor. Use a spatula to remove the mixture and press it firmly into a cake pan or brownie dish. Refrigerate for a few hours to harden the mixture and make it easier to slice and serve. Top with raw mousse for a two layer chocolate explosion.

Chia seed puddings

2 cups milk

¹/₂ cup chia seeds

2 teaspoons vanilla extract

1 tablespoon maple syrup

directions
Add all ingredients to a large jar or container with good lid. Shake vigorously for 10 seconds. Allow to set for about 30 minutes in the refrigerator, then shake vigorously again to break up any seeds that clumped together. Serve chilled.

You can have it alone or with your favorite toppings – nuts, seeds, coconut flakes, or fruit, if you don't mind the combination! This recipe keeps well in the fridge for about a week.

Chapter Thirteen

Essential Spices, Blends, and Easy Hacks

Dry Jerk Seasoning

(from *Jerk from Jamaica: Barbecue Caribbean Style* by Helen Willinsky)

1 tablespoon onion flakes

1 tablespoon onion powder

2 teaspoons ground thyme

2 teaspoons salt

1 teaspoon ground pimento (allspice)

1/4 teaspoon ground nutmeg

1/4 teaspoon ground cinnamon

2 teaspoons sugar

1 teaspoon coarsely ground black pepper

1 teaspoon cayenne pepper

2 teaspoons dried chives or green onions

directions

Add all ingredients to a jar, cover, and shake.

Tandoori Spice Mix

3 tablespoons paprika

1 tablespoon ground turmeric

1 teaspoon garlic powder

1 teaspoon ground cloves

1 teaspoon ground nutmeg

1 teaspoon cayenne pepper

1 teaspoon ground ginger

1 teaspoon ground coriander

1 teaspoon ground cumin

directions

Add all ingredients to a jar, cover, and shake.

Allergy-Sensitive Flax Milk

¹/₃ cup flax seeds

5 cups water

1 tablespoon maple syrup

directions
Combine the flax seeds and half the water in a blender. Process for a minute. Strain through a nut milk bag, or skip that step and keep the frappe-like consistency. Add remaining water and sweetener and blend for 30 seconds. Store in a pitcher in the refrigerator and use within 4 days.

Flax Eggs

These are the most gloriously healthy egg replacements that are cheap and easy.

This recipe yields the equivalent of 1 egg.

2 teaspoons flaxseed meal

3 teaspoons water

directions
Add the amount of flaxseed meal and water necessary to replace the number of eggs the recipe calls for. Whisk for a minute or so, or pulse in a blender or food processor. Let sit until it becomes gelatinous.

Easy Nut/Seed Parm

1 cup cashews (sub sunflower seeds for saving $ and allergies)

4 tablespoons nutritional yeast

1 teaspoon sea salt

1/4 teaspoon garlic powder

directions

Add all ingredients to a food processor or blender and pulse until a sandy texture is created. Store in a jar in the refrigerator for up to two weeks.

Whole Cashew Milk

This is our household favorite. After we discovered this recipe, we completely stopped buying nut milks from the store. Then, we realized maybe the kid has a slight cashew sensitivity...but up until then, it was amazing and you can help the legend live on.

1 cup raw cashews, soaked overnight and rinsed

4 cups clean water

1 tablespoon maple syrup

1 pinch sea salt

directions

Place all ingredients in a high-speed blender and liquefy on highest speed for at least one minute. No need to strain!

Keep in a pitcher in your refrigerator and consume within three days.

Allergy-Sensitive Oat Milk

I created this recipe for schools and daycares, much like my own home-based preschool, that are avoiding nuts due to allergies. It's a great use of WIC oats to create an anti-inflammatory milk source!

1 cup whole oats, soaked briefly (20 min) or overnight, and rinsed WELL

3 cups clean water

1 tablespoon maple syrup

1 teaspoon vanilla extract

1/4 teaspoon ground cinnamon

1 pinch sea salt

directions
Blend the soaked oats and water on high speed for 10 seconds.

If using a sieve: Pour the mixture into a bowl through a sieve. Pour the strained mixture back into the blender through the sieve again. If the consistency looks good, you can move to the next step. Otherwise, strain again through the sieve to remove more pulp. Add the remaining ingredients and blend to mix for a few seconds. Store in a pitcher in the refrigerator. Use within four days.

If using a nut milk bag to strain: Blend longer than 10 seconds. Squeeze the blended oats through a nut milk bag. Add the remaining ingredients and blend to mix for a few seconds. Store in a pitcher in the refrigerator. Use within four days.

Cashew Mayo

1/2 cup cashew milk

2 teaspoons lemon juice

1/2 teaspoons sea salt

1/2 teaspoon maple syrup

1/4 teaspoon ground mustard

1 cup olive oil or grapeseed oil

directions
Add all ingredients to blender except the oil. Begin blending, increasing speed, and slowly add oil. Lasts about a week, if refrigerated.

Chapter Fourteen

Zero Waste: Juicer Pulp Recipes

Carrot Crackers

Carrot Tuna

Mac and Cheese Sauce with Carrot

Veggie Broth

Carrot Crackers

1 cup carrot pulp

2 flax eggs

2 teaspoons curry

1 teaspoon smoked paprika

seasoning of your choice

1 teaspoon sea salt

1 tablespoon nutritional yeast, optional

directions
You can expand this recipe to any amount of pulp. The above amounts are general guidelines. The number of flax eggs you need for this recipe will vary depending on the volume of carrot pulp. I use two eggs per cup of carrot pulp. Mix the gelatinous flax egg in a bowl with carrot pulp. Knead in seasonings and nutritional yeast. Spoon teaspoon-size balls onto parchment or silicone liner for dehydrator. Flatten into round crackers. Dehydrate depending on your machine's instructions.

> **PRO TIP**
>
> Oven dehydration is possible. Use your oven on lowest setting (180°F) and bake for about 20 minutes.

Carrot Tuna

3-5 cups carrot pulp, or mixed celery and carrot pulp

2 sticks of celery, diced

$^1/_2$ red onion, diced

juice of 1 lemon

1 cup cashew mayo or mayo of your choice

1 tablespoon dulse flakes or powder, optional

directions
Mix all ingredients until thoroughly combined. Serve as topping on a salad or enjoy as a meal.

Mac and Cheese Sauce with Carrot

1 cup carrot pulp

1 cup soaked cashews (sub one avocado for nut allergy)

1 red bell pepper, deseeded, destemmed, and quartered

3 sun-dried tomatoes, soaked in hot water if stored without oil

1 garlic clove

2 tablespoons good oil

2 tablespoons nutritional yeast

1 teaspoon sea salt, more or less to taste

$1/4$ teaspoon ground white pepper

clean water to adjust consistency, as needed

directions
Blend all ingredients until smooth. Add water slowly to adjust consistency. Serve over hot cooked pasta.

MORE WAYS TO USE JUICER PULP

Coleslaw (use carrot pulp instead of shredded carrot), see Jerk Coleslaw and Carrot Coconut Slaw
in *Chapter Eight - Roughage.*

Veggie Burgers
(Chapter Eleven – Protein Finale)

Stuffing for Sticky Rice Buns
(Chapter Ten – Cooked Grains)

Veggie Broth

3-6 cups assorted veggie pulp, depending on what will fit in your Crock-Pot or soup pot

1-2 inches of kombu seaweed

Irish moss jelly, optional

directions

Use the juicer pulp without the fruit ingredients if possible. Celery, carrots, greens, ginger, and/or fennel make for a tasty broth.

Submerge pulp in clean water with a 1 inch strip of kombu. If you don't have kombu, it is fine to brew this broth with another kind of seaweed like wakame or hijiki. Steep on warm setting of crock pot overnight.

Alternately you can cook it on low in the crock pot for a few hours, or boil gently in a dutch oven on the stove top for an hour and let steep for another hour.

After cooling, pour liquid through a strainer into another clean pot or bowl. Press on the pulp in the strainer to release more broth with the back of a spoon or your hand.

I use a nut milk bag to strain and then squeeze all the liquid from the stewed pulp. If you add Irish moss jelly and blend with an immersion blender you will have a collagen-boosting vegan "bone broth" on your hands.

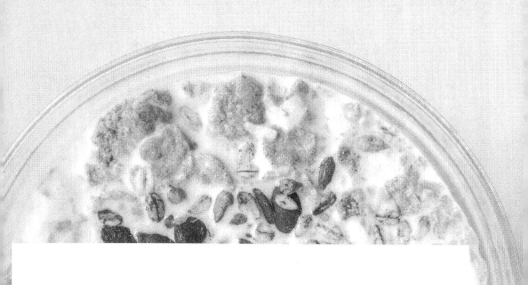

Chapter Fifteen

Oh Shit Survival Guide:
Cabbage and Sunflower Seeds

There may come a day in your life, if it hasn't already come, when you say, "Oh Shit! Holy Mother of God! I am too broke to buy ANYTHING!!!" Don't despair, this is totally temporary, and can be your chance to seriously clean up your diet. My master teacher, Gil, always reminds me of cabbage and sunflower seeds. These two items, possibly the cheapest whole foods in the grocery store, will nourish you and keep you fed for the least investment. Check out the options for preparing them. Also make sure you refer to some of my strategies to get creative ways to acquire more food for free (*Chapter Five – Friends With Benefits*).

> **...cabbage and sunflower seeds... These two items, possibly the cheapest... will nourish you and keep you fed for the least investment.**

Boiled Cabbage

This is the most simple yet delicious recipe from my childhood. A simple green cabbage cooked down into a soft soothing dish, can increase the size of any meal as a side dish, and can itself be enjoyed as a meal.

1 cabbage, sliced thinly around stalky areas

1 cup water

salt and pepper, to taste

directions
Add all ingredients to a sauce pan, cover, bring to a boil, and reduce to low. Add more water if necessary. However, it is best to wait for the cabbage to release its water while being cooked to avoid diluting the taste.

Simmer on low until desired consistency is reached. Season to your liking.

Habesha Cabbage

1 cabbage, chopped

1 onion, diced

1 tomato, diced

$^1/_2$ cup water

$^1/_2$ can of 6 ounces
tomato paste or about 2
tablespoons,optional

1 tablespoon oil

1-2 jalapeño or chili
peppers,optional

3 garlic cloves, pressed

1 inch ginger, peeled and
chopped finely

1 teaspoon sea salt

2 teaspoons berbere, optional
(The recipe tastes good even
without this quintessential
East African spice blend.)

directions
Heat oil and sauté onions
with sea salt. Add garlic
and ginger and cook until
pungent. Add diced tomato
and allow to cook on
medium for 5-10 minutes.

Mix in tomato paste and
berbere. Add chopped
cabbage and whole peppers
and coat with the tomato/
onion sauce.

Add water and cover. Bring
to a boil and reduce to low,
stirring occasionally. Turn
off heat after the thicker
cabbage pieces soften. Stir
and leave covered as cabbage
softens to perfect texture.

*Serve with injera if you are so
blessed to have some. This dish
is also good with rice or bread.*

Cabbage Wraps

6 leaves of green or Napa
cabbage

1-2 cups of sunflower
seed pâté (*Chapter Eight -
Roughage*)

directions
Prepare pâté. Scoop pâté into

the center of the leaf, if it is
small; fold and eat taco style. If
it is a larger leaf, try scooping
the pâté onto the leaf and
spreading somewhat evenly.
Roll the leaf tightly, then
slice like sushi rolls. Top
with Un-peanut Sauce
(*Chapter Eight - Roughage*).

Cabbage Salad

green and red cabbage

your favorite dressing

sunflower seed pâté (*Chapter Eight - Roughage*)

directions
Any amount of green and red cabbage plus your favorite dressing and sunflower seed pâté from *Chapter Eight – Roughage*.

Broth Soup with Veggies

We love making this easy soup when we feel like soothing our souls after a long day or while sick. Issa named the dish "broth soup" because it is almost completely veggie stock. Use my veggie broth recipe in *Chapter Fourteen - Zero Waste*, or buy cheap store-brand liters to have on hand. You can also make a broth out of miso paste (fermented soybeans) and there's also chickpea miso, which we keep around for easy seasoning. Miso is super flavorful, and available for cheap at Asian markets and most conventional grocery stores as well.

1 liter veggie broth or 1 liter water plus 2 tablespoons miso paste

$^1/_4$ cabbage, shredded

tamari/soy or salt, to taste

1 tablespoon oil (sesame, coconut, and avocado have worked well)

hot sauce, optional

$^1/_3$ cup any veggies on hand, sliced thinly

1 package of the last bag of rice noodles hiding out in your food stash, optional

directions
If using noodles, cook according to instructions. Add stock or water without miso to a medium sauce pan. If using miso for broth, it will be added in the final step.

Add all cabbage, veggie slices, and seasonings to a pot and bring to a boil. Cover and cook on low until softened (about 10 minutes).

Add miso paste which you made into liquid form by following the pro tip, and mix well. Add oil before serving.

Sunflower Seed Butter

1 cup sunflower seeds (will
be different for raw, roasted,
and salted: all work well)

¹/₂ cup sunflower oil

¹/₄ cup maple syrup

directions
Add all ingredients to food
processor with S blade. I had moderate success with
a blender, and the magic
bullet nut/seed grinder
attachment was somewhat
successful. Pulse until well.
Scrape down edges of food
processor periodically. You
may need to add more oil for
smoother processing. Do so
sparingly.

Baked Sunflower Seed Meat

Use the pâté recipe (*Chapter Eight - Roughage*) or try a
variation of the pâté combined with whatever herbs and
spices you have on hand. I originally created this for stuffed
peppers, so I suggest snagging a couple vibrantly colored
bell peppers if that is within your survival budget.

1 sunflower seed pâté recipe
(*Chapter Eight - Roughage*)

2 red bell peppers

directions
Slice each pepper in half,
remove seeds, and fill with
sunflower seed pâté.

*Optionally, you may layer
thinly sliced veggies within the
pepper and pâté.*

Bake for 20 minutes on
400°F on a baking sheet or
any oven-safe pan. Allow to
cool and settle for 5 minutes
before serving.

MORE OH SHIT
SURVIVAL RECIPES

Jerk Coleslaw (*Chapter Eight - Roughage*)

DIY Sauerkraut (Google that)

Sunflower Seed Pâté (*Chapter Eight - Roughage*)

Appendix A
Shopping Lists

Sample Shopping Lists for Your Radical Budget: Bottomless Shopping List

The best way to keep abundant and fresh food items in your house for use at any given moment is to follow these guidelines for shopping. In this practice of eating and consuming, you are learning which food items offer essential nutrients, and which products have been marketed to you as healthy options that may have little benefit to you as a human, while offering huge profits to food companies. One difference you may notice is that while you are likely to spend less on groceries now that you have sorted out the unnecessaries, you may be heading to the store or produce stand more often than before. This is usually a good sign, since fresher, nutrient-dense food has a very short shelf life, and you are eating a lot more of it.

Fresh Produce Essentials

- Coconut water liters
- Aloe vera gel
- Coconut oil, grapeseed oil, sunflower seed oil
- Toasted sesame oil
- Raw almond butters
- Raw tahini
- Roasted nut and seed butters
- Soy or coconut aminos (Braggs or Coconut Secret brands)
- Raw apple cider vinegar
- Wheat-free tamari (soy sauce)
- Nori wraps
- Frozen potatoes and sweet potato fries
- Manna bread and sprouted breads stored in freezer
- Seaweed snacks
- Veggie chips, Snapea Crisps, Inner Peas, plantain chips
- Kettle cooked potato chips
- Honey or maple syrup for vegans
- Soy-free Earth Balance buttery spread or coconut butter-based spread
- Dairy-free dark chocolate
- Carob, cacao, cocoa powder
- Coconut milk ice cream
- Gluten-free grains, stored properly
- Bulk beans, stored properly
- Sea salt
- Cinnamon
- Turmeric
- Cardamom
- Non-toxic seasoning
- Nutritional Yeast
- Dulse powder
- Greens powder like Vitamineral Green and Green Vibrance

Appendix B
Storage Guide

How to Store Your Food So it Lasts and You Save Dough

	How to Keep	*When to Replace*
Sugar	In plastic, glass, or ceramic sealed container in refrigerator	Discard if showing signs of infestation or black bugs
Rice, grains	In airtight glass containers	Can keep in fridge for up to a year; discard if showing signs of infestation
Nuts, seeds	In airtight jars	Keep in refrigerator or freezer if not consumed within two weeks
Flours	In plastic bags in freezer	If frozen, dispose after 1-2 years, or if showing signs of infestation or mold when not stored properly
Dry Beans	In airtight glass containers	If frozen, dispose after 1-2 years, or if showing signs of infestation or mold when not stored properly
Bread	In plastic bag, sealed in refrigerator	Discard if molding

	How to Keep	When to Replace
Cookies, crackers	In airtight glass containers / cookie jars	Most fresh-baked products go bad after 3-4 days. Boxed varieties may have a longer shelf life.
Bananas	Allow to ripen in a fruit dish, but after a day or once ripe, peel and freeze if you won't be eating them immediately	
General fruit	Once ripe, move to crisper drawer of refrigerator	
Leafy greens, herbs	Wash and store with a wet paper towel inside a plastic bag. Seal the bag and keep in refrigerator.	Depending on freshness when purchased, most veggies are only good for 5-7 days in the fridge.
Potatoes	In a plastic bag in refrigerator	Discard when sprouting from ears. Contains toxins.
Onions	They are fine outside in the kitchen, but last longer and are easier to chop when refrigerated	Discard when decaying or sprouting
Dry spices	In glass containers in cool dark cabinets	They lose potency after 6 months
Oils	Keep olive oil shielded from light in a tinted jar or dark cabinet. Keep coconut oil cool in fridge on hot days.	Discard if taste changes, or after 6 months to a year.

Appendix C
Money-Saving Products
You Can Make with Food (Stamps)

General

Baking soda cleansers
for hair and skin

Apple cider vinegar diluted in water
for hair conditioner and skin tonic

Baking soda-based toothpaste and deodorant
for toothpaste: add xylitol, coconut oil, and mint; for deodorant: add coconut, shea and arrowroot

Coffee, sugar, and salt
for body scrubs

Honey, banana, or avocado
for hair and skin conditioners

Egg whites plus lime juice
for dandruff

EBT Medicine Cabinet

Coconut oil
for skin and hair care

Chamomile tea infusion
for anxiety and digestive stress

Lavender infusion
for nervousness

Corn silk infusion or cranberry juice
for urinary tract infections

Apple cider vinegar
for fungus

Baking soda
for acid reflux

Aloe vera
for acid reflux

Appendix D
Tools to Manifest

- Veggie peeler
- Garlic press
- Ice cream scoop with spring (good for making neat rice scoops or measuring out cookie dough)
- Handheld spiralizer
- Shaking jar (can be any glass mason jar that seals)
- Citrus press
- Whisk
- Hi-speed blender
- Juicer (used Brevilles and Omegas are easy to find online)
- Cutting boards
- Good knife (I use one knife for almost everything.)
- 2 cast iron skillets
- Cast-iron or enamel dutch oven

AUTHOR BIO

Rachel Bolden-Kramer is a writer and baby momma revolutionary originally from San Francisco's Haight Ashbury neighborhood. She disturbed the status-quo as a militant teenager and poetry slam champion in the 1990s. Rachel credits the arts and activism movement of her generation in the Bay Area for contributing to her keen sense of creative justice.

Rachel is a first-generation graduate of Harvard University where she wrote extensively about race, gender, and class (obviously). While completing her senior honors thesis on Vogue Balls and queer youth of color, she became acutely aware of the role of food and nutrition in self-determination. This awareness of the transformative power of food and lifestyle choices lead her to become a Registered Yoga Teacher (Spirit Rock Meditation Center, Yoga Alliance, Niroga Institute) and radical nutritionist (Center for Mind Body Medicine). Her studies in yoga, mindfulness, and nutritional healing proved invaluable when faced with the experiences of violence and intergenerational trauma in the United States.

Rachel became an expert in navigating the public assistance system while healing a complex trauma, and later referenced her strategies for survival at the margins in her workshops on radical healing commissioned by the New York City Housing Authority. The early "My Food Stamps Cookbook" workshops grew into the Hip Dhamma Yoga Studio of Brooklyn, a community center for healing, owned and operated by Black Women yoga teachers in Bedford-Stuyvesant.

Rachel returned to the Bay Area after the home birth of her Bodhisattva baby, Issa, and developed a holistic childcare and preschool company based on the wisdom of attachment parenting. She derives immense joy from supporting families as a doula and childcare provider, while expanding the reach of the My Food Stamps Cookbook revolution! In May 2017, over 1000 backers made the cookbook become a reality in print and ebook via Kickstarter and Backerkit crowdsourcing.

MY FOOD STAMPS COOKBOOK INDEX

Made in the USA
San Bernardino, CA
03 May 2018